WHAT IS OPUS DEI?

Blessed Josemaría Escrivá

What is
Opus Dei?

Dominique le Tourneau

JOSEMARÍA ESCRIVÁ
CENTENARY OF HIS BIRTH

GRACEWING

First published in English in 1987 jointly by
The Mercier Press Ltd, Dublin
and Fowler Wright Books Ltd, Leominster

This edition published in 2001

Gracewing
2 Southern Avenue, Leominster
Herefordshire HR6 0QF

Translated from *L'Opus Dei*
© Presses Universitaires de France 1984

Nihil obstat: Stephen J. Greene, censor deputatus.
Imprimi potest: + Joseph A. Carroll, Diocesan Administrator,
10 August 1987.
(The Nihil obstat and Imprimi potest are a declaration that a book
or publication is considered to be free from doctrinal or moral
error. This declaration does not imply approval of, or agreement
with, the contents, opinions or statements expressed.)

ISBN 0 85244 136 3

Typeset by Action Publishing Technology Ltd,
Gloucester, GL1 5SR

Printed in England by Antony Rowe Ltd,
Chippenham SN14 6LH

Contents

Historical overview

1928. *2 October*: While on a spiritual retreat in Madrid, Blessed Josemaría Escrivá, under divine inspiration, founded Opus Dei as a way of sanctification for people from all walks of life, in their daily work and the fulfilment of their ordinary duties as Christians. The name 'Opus Dei' came later and was not used until the early 1930s. However, from the outset, in his writings and conversations about what God was asking of him, he would talk of the *Work of God*.

1930. *14 February*: In Madrid, while celebrating Mass, God enabled Blessed Josemaría to understand that the message of Opus Dei was addressed to women as well.

1933. The first centre of Opus Dei was opened in Madrid: the DYA Academy, mainly for students, where classes in law and architecture were given.

1934. DYA became a residence for college students. From that base the founder and the first members offered Christian formation, and spread the message of Opus Dei among young people. An important aspect of this work was the teaching of the Catholic faith to children, and looking after the poor and sick in the outlying neighbourhoods of Madrid. Fr. Josemaría made his activity known at all times to the bishop of Madrid, who from the very beginning granted his approval and blessing. *Consideraciones espirituales*, the forerunner of *The Way*, was published.

1936. The Spanish Civil War: religious persecution was unleashed and Fr. Josemaría was obliged to hide in various different places. This interruption of his apostolic work temporarily delayed the plans of the founder to expand the apostolic work of Opus Dei to other countries.

1937. The founder and some members of Opus Dei completed a harrowing escape over the Pyrenees through Andorra and made their way to an area where the Church was not being persecuted (Burgos).

1938. Renewal of apostolic work in Burgos, Spain.

1939. Fr. Josemaría returned to Madrid. Expansion of Opus Dei to other Spanish cities. The beginning of World War II prevented expansion to other countries.

1941. *19 March*: The bishop of Madrid, Leopoldo Eijo y Garay, granted the first diocesan approval of Opus Dei.

1943. *14 February*: Again during Mass, God let Fr. Josemaría see the juridical solution that would enable priests to be ordained for Opus Dei: the Priestly Society of the Holy Cross.

1944. *25 June*: The bishop of Madrid ordained three members of Opus Dei as priests: Alvaro del Portillo, José María Hernández de Garnica, and José Luis Múzquiz.

1946. The founder of Opus Dei moved to Rome. In the years that followed, he would travel from Rome throughout Europe to prepare the beginnings of the work of Opus Dei in several different countries.

1947. *24 February*: The Holy See granted the first pontifical approval.

1948. *29 June*: The founder established the Roman College of the Holy Cross, where from that time on, numerous members of Opus Dei would study and receive a deep spiritual and pastoral formation, while taking courses at various pontifical teaching establishments in Rome.

1950. *16 June*: Pius XII granted the definitive approval to Opus Dei. This approval enabled married people to join Opus Dei, and secular clergy to be admitted to the Priestly Society of the Holy Cross.

1952. The University of Navarre was begun at Pamplona, Spain.

1953. *12 December*: The Roman College of Our Lady was established to provide an intense spiritual, theological and apostolic formation for women of Opus Dei from all over the world.

1957. The Holy See entrusted the prelature of Yauyos, a mountainous region of Peru, to Opus Dei.

1965. *21 November*: Paul VI inaugurated the ELIS Centre, a vocational training centre for young people located in an industrial sector of Rome, together with a parish entrusted to Opus Dei by the Holy See.

1969. A special general congress of Opus Dei met in Rome to study the change of Opus Dei's legal status in the Church to that of a personal prelature, a juridical structure introduced by the Second Vatican Council and ideally suited to the pastoral characteristics of Opus Dei.

1970. The founder of Opus Dei travelled to Mexico. He prayed for nine days at the shrine of Our Lady of Guadalupe, and addressed large groups of people on topics affecting their Christian life. This was the first of what he called his catechetical journeys.

1972. Mgr. Josemaría Escrivá travelled throughout Spain and Portugal on a catechetical journey lasting two months.

1974. Catechetical journey of the founder to six South American countries: Brazil, Argentina, Chile, Peru, Ecuador and Venezuela.

1975. Catechetical journey of the founder to Venezuela and Guatemala.

26 June: Josemaría Escrivá died in Rome. Some 60,000 people belonged to Opus Dei at that time.

7 July: Inauguration of the new shrine of Our Lady of Torreciudad in Huesca, Spain.

15 September: Alvaro del Portillo was elected to succeed the founder at a congress of Opus Dei members called for that purpose, as required by canon law.

1982. *28 November*: John Paul II established Opus Dei as a personal prelature, a juridical structure more accurately reflecting Opus Dei's theological and pastoral nature, and appointed Mgr. Alvaro del Portillo as prelate.

1983. *19 March*: Formal execution of the apostolic constitution establishing Opus Dei as a personal prelature.

1985. Inauguration of the Roman Academic Centre of the Holy Cross, which in 1998 would become the Pontifical University of the Holy Cross.

1991. *6 January*: John Paul II ordained Mgr. Alvaro del Portillo as bishop.

1992. *17 May*: Beatification of Josemaría Escrivá in St Peter's Square in Rome.

1994. *23 March*: Death of Bishop Alvaro del Portillo in Rome just hours after his return from a trip to the Holy Land.

20 April: Mgr. Javier Echevarría was appointed as prelate of Opus Dei by John Paul II, confirming the election carried out by the general elective congress held in Rome.

1995. *6 January*: Mgr. Javier Echevarría was ordained bishop by John Paul II.

Dates on which Opus Dei began its work in different countries

1946 Portugal, Italy, Great Britain
1947 France, Ireland
1949 Mexico, United States
1950 Chile, Argentina
1951 Colombia, Venezuela

1952 Germany
1953 Guatemala, Peru
1954 Ecuador
1956 Uruguay, Switzerland
1957 Brazil, Austria, Canada
1958 Japan, Kenya, El Salvador
1959 Costa Rica, Holland
1962 Paraguay
1963 Australia
1964 Philippines
1965 Belgium, Nigeria
1969 Puerto Rico
1978 Bolivia
1980 Congo, Ivory Coast, Honduras
1981 Hong Kong
1982 Singapore
1983 Trinidad and Tobago
1984 Sweden
1985 Taiwan
1987 Finland
1988 Cameroon, Dominican Republic
1989 Macao, New Zealand, Poland
1990 Hungary, Czech Republic
1992 Nicaragua
1993 India, Israel
1994 Lithuania
1996 Estonia, Slovakia, Lebanon, Panama, Uganda
1997 Kazakhstan
1998 South Africa

Blessed Josemaría with Fr. Alvaro del Portillo (left) and Fr. Javier Echevarría outside the Church of St Dunstan in Canterbury, where the head of St Thomas More is buried. Blessed Josemaría was very devoted to St Thomas More, and he was able to visit his tomb during his summer visits to England between 1958 and 1962.

This photo was taken on 26 August 1958. Fr. Alvaro del Portillo succeeded Blessed Josemaría as head of Opus Dei when the founder died in 1975. He was consecrated Bishop by Pope John Paul II in 1991 and died in 1994. Bishop Javier Echevarría is the current Prelate of Opus Dei.

Note to the Second English Edition

The year 2002 marks the centenary of the birth of Josemaría Escrivá, founder of Opus Dei. Since the first English edition of this book in 1984 the most significant development has been the beatification of Blessed Josemaría Escrivá on 17 May 1992 by Pope John Paul II.

Mgr. Alvaro del Portillo, who was Prelate of Opus Dei at the date of the first English edition, was ordained Bishop in January 1991. He died in 1994, and Pope John Paul II appointed as his successor Mgr. Javier Echevarría, who was then ordained Bishop on 6 January 1995.

Since 1984 the apostolic work of Opus Dei has started in 20 new countries including Finland, Poland, Hungary, Nicaragua, Israel, Uganda, Kazakhstan and South Africa.

Pope Paul VI says goodbye to the founder after the Pope had officially opened the ELIS Centre in Rome in 1965. Pope Paul said of Opus Dei that it had 'arisen in our times as an expression of the perennial youth of the church.'

The ELIS Centre, in the working class Tiburtino district, was built with the help and encouragement of Pope John XXIII. Run by members of Opus Dei, it comprises a hostel for 140 apprentices and young workers, a technical school, a secondary school and a sports centre.

See page 89–90 for details.

Introduction

The Prelature of the Holy Cross and Opus Dei, better known simply as Opus Dei, 'has arisen in our time as a living expression of the perennial youthfulness of the Church, which is fully open to the demands of today's apostolate' (Pope Paul VI). It proclaims that lay people can and ought to seek holiness in the context of their ordinary life, through the free and responsible exercise of their everyday work, and through an apostolate carried out within the ordinary structures of society, in response to a genuine vocation from God. Since 2 October 1928 – the date of its foundation – this has been the message of Opus Dei, the hallmark of its spirituality, lived by people of every race and social background.

This book takes a look at the lifestyle of members of Opus Dei; it describes their apostolic activities, at the personal level and in association with others; it studies the statutes of the Prelature and the writings of its founder, Monsignor Escrivá, including some hitherto unpublished material. (All my quotations are from him, unless otherwise referenced.) It begins with a short account of the founder's life.

I have tried to identify the main features of Opus Dei and the kind of contribution it might be expected to make in building a more Christian world.

1: Blessed Josemaría Escrivá

FIRST INTIMATIONS

Childhood

Josemaría Escrivá was born on 9 January 1902 in Barbastro in Northern Spain. He was the second in a family of six children. His father ran a retail business with two associates, selling chocolate and textiles. His mother, second youngest in a family of thirteen, was of French descent. Both parents gave their home an atmosphere of solid piety, devoid of intolerance, and their children received a good training in human virtues. The Escrivás had more than their share of set-backs: they had to endure the death of their three youngest daughters in the space of just three years, the bankruptcy of Mr Escrivá's business and his having to take a new job away from their home in Logroño.

Josemaría started school when he was three. During his teens he became very well read – well above the level needed for his second-level exams: he was particularly keen on history and read many classical works of literature. Throughout his life he could quote Spanish and foreign writers with ease.

First intimations

In December 1917, when he was almost sixteen, a small incident made a strong impression on the young Josemaría. The family were living in Logroño at the time. It had been snowing. Making his way along his usual route Josemaría came across the freshly-made imprints of the bare feet of a discalced Carmelite monk. A certain restlessness arose in his heart. He began to sense that God was expecting something particular of him, but he didn't know precisely what. He later described these feelings as 'the first

10

inklings of Love'. He decided to go to Holy Communion every day and to improve his life of piety and penance. He often repeated the cry of the blind man of Jericho to Jesus, 'Domine, ut videam!' (Lord, make me see!)

Priest

He made up his mind then to give up the idea he had of becoming an architect. He decided he would be a priest, hoping that that would make it easier for him to fulfil that will of God, as yet unknown to him.

In 1918 he began his studies for the priesthood in the seminary of Logroño and in 1920 went on to the one in Saragossa. There he attracted the attention of the archbishop, Cardinal Soldevila, who in 1922 appointed him a superior of the seminary. Constantly seeking to see his way more clearly, he spent long nights in prayer.

Parallel with his last years of theology studies, Josemaría began a course in civil law, putting in a lot of work during the holidays. He was ordained on 28 March 1925. His father had died four months earlier at the age of fifty-seven, worn out by work.

Fr. Escrivá's first appointment was as a temporary curate in a poor country parish. In May 1925 he returned to Saragossa; his pastoral duties included giving catechism classes in the surrounding district, visiting poor families, looking after a church, and helping his brothers in the priesthood. At the same time he continued studying for his law degree and carried out apostolate with his fellow-students at the university. He also gave classes in Latin and canon law: he was now the head of the family and had to earn money to provide for his mother, his older sister and his youngest brother.

In March 1927 he obtained leave to move to Madrid to study for a doctorate in civil law. He spent a lot of his time going from one end of the city to the other, offering his priestly services to the sick in hospital, to the poor, and to children who had either been abandoned or who came from very poor families; every year he prepared thousands of them for their first confession and first Holy Communion. He became chaplain to the Association of the Sick, a charitable work for the assistance and instruction of the destitute. He continued to give classes in civil law and in canon law. He worked a long, tiring day; he spent long periods in prayer, had an ardent devotion to the Blessed Virgin and did rigorous corporal mortification. With this kind of lifestyle he hoped that God would show him what direction his life should take.

FOUNDATION YEARS

The founding of Opus Dei

On 2 October 1928 during a retreat, Fr. Escrivá 'saw' – the term he later used – what God was expecting of him. He saw that our Lord was asking him to devote all his energy to accomplishing what was to become Opus Dei; to urge men in all walks of life – beginning with university people so as afterwards to be able to reach all men – to respond to a specific vocation to seek holiness and carry out apostolate in the midst of the world, through the exercise of their profession or trade, without a change of state.

From this point on Fr. Escrivá never had a moment's 'tranquillity'; he set about his new work without giving up any of his previous responsibilities. He had no financial resources; his only equipment, as he put it, was 'twenty-six years of age, God's grace, and a good sense of humour'. Once more he went in search of the strength he needed among 'the incurably sick, the poor people rejected by everyone, homeless children with nobody to give them any instruction, in homes without fires, without warmth, and without love'. Here again he personally looked after thousands of souls every year. He also engaged in a letter-writing apostolate with all types of people including priests.

A few days after he had written, 'There will never be any

women in Opus Dei, no fear!' on 14 February 1930 a new, divine inspiration from God made him realise that he had to spread the message of holiness in the middle of the world to women as well as men. From then on Opus Dei had two sections, one for men and one for women, inspired by the same spirit.

At the outset this 'apostolic work' didn't even have a name. One day a friend of his asked him, 'How is that work of God coming along?' A name had been found: the work of God, *Opus Dei, operatio Dei*, God's work, ordinary work transformed into prayer along all the paths of the world.

Development of apostolic work

The founder did his apostolate wherever he possibly could – in hospitals, in chapels, in offices, in the university, etc. Some vocations materialised, although souls also slipped away 'like eels'. At the end of 1933 he opened the DYA Academy (named after the initials of the Spanish for 'Law and Architecture'), which was the first group initiative of Opus Dei. Despite all kinds of financial difficulties his apostolic zeal remained buoyant. The following year the Academy moved to more spacious premises, and a residence for students was added. All this was to be destroyed during the Spanish Civil War. In fact, one of the first incidents involving bloodshed took place nearby, at the Montaña Barracks.

Religious persecution during the Civil War meant that Fr. Escrivá had to go into hiding and keep moving from one refuge to the next, until eventually, in March 1937, he found a place in the Honduras consulate. At the risk of his life he regularly used to leave the consulate to do a very extensive priestly work.

His sons, the first members of the Work, eventually convinced him to leave the Republican zone. In November and December 1937, with some of them, he undertook a hazardous crossing of the Pyrenees, ill-equipped and in bitter weather. After fourteen days they reached Andorra and then returned to Spain via Lourdes. The first thing Fr. Escrivá did on arrival was to go on retreat, after which he resumed his apostolic work in Burgos. He re-established contact with everyone he had known before the outbreak of hostilities.

At the end of the Civil War he went back to Madrid. Within five months he had already set up a new residence for students. Since he was the only priest in Opus Dei he had to look after the formation of new vocations and take care of the residence. In addition he was chaplain to the St. Elizabeth Foundation, a convent of enclosed Augustinian nuns. He gave spiritual direction to hundreds of people, men and women, married and single, students, teachers, writers, workers, etc. He organised retreats and days of recollection. He also set about the expansion of Opus Dei, leaving by train late on Saturday afternoons for Valencia, Barcelona, Salamanca, etc., returning on the Sunday on a night train. At the request of many bishops he gave retreats to diocesan clergy (during one of which he was to hear of the unexpected death of his mother). He also preached to many committees of religious, both men and women.

This intense activity during the 1940s took place against a background of criticism from a number of clerics who, no doubt in good faith, regarded him as unorthodox for preaching a vocation to sanctity in the middle of the world. However, the bishop of Madrid, fully aware of the spirit, aims and methods of Opus Dei (he had encouraged Fr. Escrivá from the very beginning, and blessed his Work), did everything possible to defend him. It was he who, on 25 June 1944, ordained the first three priest members of Opus Dei.

For some time the founder had been trying to work out how to have priests in Opus Dei. During Mass on 14 February 1943 he saw the solution: it would be through the ordination of lay members. Since they would have the same spirit they would be in a good position to provide the precise formation required; would make it much easier for the apostolate to expand, and would help ensure that the true spirit of Opus Die was preserved and developed. Thus the Priestly Society of the Holy Cross was born. It represented a new *pastoral* phenomenon in the Church (men with university degrees and already practising a profession 'who, without expecting anything in return, give themselves to serve all souls, especially their brothers'), and it was also something of a new *juridical* development (the fact of becoming a priest within Opus Dei does not involve a change in God's calling to respond, with the greatest possible perfection, to the Christian vocation to sanctity).

Crossing all frontiers

The Spanish Civil War, and then the Second World War, prevented the spread of Opus Dei to other countries. In 1953 Fr. Escrivá had envisaged sending some of his sons to Paris; but this project had to be postponed because of adverse circumstances. As soon as it became possible, at the end of the Second World War, little by little members of the Work began to go to other countries: Portugal, and shortly afterwards England and Italy (1946), France and Ireland (1947), Argentina (1950), Colombia and Venezuela (1951), Germany (1952), Peru and Guatemala (1953), Ecuador (1954), Uruguay and Switzerland (1956), Brazil, Austria and Canada (1957), El Salvador, Kenya and Japan (1958), Costa Rica and Holland (1959), Paraguay (1962), Australia (1963), the Philippines (1964), Nigeria and Belgium (1965), Puerto Rico (1969).

The founder followed the beginnings in each country very closely. Often all he could send his children off with was a blessing and a picture of our Lady. They had to sort things out for themselves with the help of the grace of God . . . He did nevertheless journey throughout Europe preparing the ground and giving encouragement to his sons and daughters in the different places.

At the end of 1946 he moved to Rome to be at the centre of Christianity, close to the Vicar of Christ, and thereby to underline the universal character of Opus Dei. In 1948 he set up the Roman College of the Holy Cross for the training of members of the men's section, who came from the different countries the Work had spread to. In 1953 he established the Roman College of our Lady for the women's section.

From Rome Mgr. Escrivá, appointed a domestic prelate to there

Pope in 1947, encouraged and directed apostolic activities of every description which members organised; he governed Opus Dei with the help of a council for each section. He also received a large number of people who came to see him and seek his counsel, Catholics, Christians of other denominations, Jews, agnostics . . .

He also accepted certain papal appointments as a member of a Pontifical Academy of Theology (1957), as a consultor to the Sacred Congregation for Seminaries (1957), and to the Pontifical Commission for the Interpretation of the Code of Canon Law (1961).

Mgr. Escrivá suffered a great deal on account of the doctrinal confusion spread in the Church by misinterpretations of the teaching of Vatican II. He went on penitential pilgrimages to various Marian shrines, including our Lady of Pilar, and our Lady of Torreciudad (Spain), Fatima, Guadalupe (Mexico), Loreto, Lourdes, Aparecida (Brazil) and Lujan (Argentina). On these occasions he addressed catechetical meetings in which he spoke about God to large audiences, sometimes of several thousand people. At these meetings he answered people's questions on such subjects as apostolate, family life, the meanings of suffering, and education. In 1970 he visited Mexico, and in 1972 travelled throughout Spain and Portugal for two months, meeting more than 150,000 people. From May to August 1974 he journeyed through six countries in South America; in February 1975 he returned to that continent. In this way more than a million people were able to hear him.

On 28 March 1975 Mgr. Escrivá de Balaguer celebrated the golden anniversary of his ordination to the priesthood; this celebration was, in accordance with his preference, a private affair. As he put it, 'my role is to pass unnoticed and disappear, so that only Jesus is in the limelight'. (His journeys abroad had been an exception in a life entirely dedicated to his priestly ministry and to his work of directing Opus Dei.)

On 23 May he visited the shrine of our Lady of Torreciudad (in northern Spain) a shrine which he himself had developed out of gratitude to the Blessed Virgin. There he used the same prayer he had used when he had sensed the first intimations of his vocation 'Domine ut videam!' (Lord, make me see!) expressing now his desire to see God face to face.

He died suddenly on 26 June 1975, in Rome, just after entering the office where he worked.

A normal day during Mgr. Escrivá's years in Rome

As soon as he got up Mgr. Escrivá would kiss the floor, saying 'Serviam' (I will serve!) as a way of offering his whole day to God, and then he used to say some prayers he had learned from his mother. He then spent half an hour in mental prayer. In this way he prepared for Mass which he said with very great devotion and which he extended into a period of thanksgiving afterwards. Before beginning his work he said his breviary. This was immediately followed by office work and correspondence. At the end of the morning he usually received visitors, after which he would spend a few moments in the oratory. At midday he said the Angelus. Every day he read a passage from Sacred Scripture and did some spiritual reading. He also kept up his study of the sacred sciences and his general reading.

He ate very frugally but he was careful to conceal his austerity whenever he had guests. Sometimes when alone he observed a total fast. Immediately after lunch he would pay a short visit to our Lord in the oratory, something which he also used to do frequently throughout the day.

Before beginning work again in the afternoon he would spend half an hour chatting with his sons in a family get-together. He said all three parts of the rosary, spread conveniently throughout the day, and spent another half-hour in mental prayer at a fixed time in the afternoon.

In the evening after another get-together with his sons he would retire in silence to do a short examination of conscience and say some last prayers. He would go to sleep saying spiritual communions, aspirations, and so on.

The man

Numerous documents and testimonies covering the entire life of
the founder allow us to learn a lot about what kind of person he
was. People outside Opus Dei considered him a man of excep-
tional intelligence: his results at school, at the seminary and at
university were with very few exceptions outstanding. His teachings show his training as a civil and canon lawyer. His capacity for
understanding and resolving problems and his knowledge of man
and of affairs were profound. He had a rare gift for foreseeing the
trend of future events.

The Jewish psychiatrist Victor Frankl said he was fascinated by
'the refreshing serenity which emanated from him and warmed
our whole conversation; then, by the unbelievable rhythm and
flow of his thoughts; and finally by his remarkable ability to establish direct contact in conversation with people', whether with an
individual person or before a vast audience, whether with blue
collar workers or academics, children or adults, Peruvian farm
labourers, or South American Indians.

His affection went out to everyone, even to anticlerical people
and people hostile to his work. Everyone came away with the
impression that he had nothing else to do but to be with them.
Even many years after the event he could recall the tiniest details
about people, their names, their relatives, and their family affairs.

His contagious joy and cheerfulness put everybody at their
ease. If someone was sick he would spend long periods at his
bedside cheering him up and helping him to pray. If he was
receiving a visitor or was with a group of people, he would always
make sure they had a pleasant time, even if he were seriously ill
himself or had passed a sleepless night.

If he really had to reprimand someone – something he could do
very effectively if need be – he felt it more than the person
corrected, and would invariably include some kind touch which,
without taking anything away from the reprimand, made it much
easier to accept.

He used to give himself no importance and spoke of himself

with humility and simplicity, immediately re-directing compliments he received to God. His capacity for work and his organisational ability meant that he made very good use of his time; he really applied himself to whatever he was doing down to the last detail. His writings show a cultured mind, a knowledge of history and literature, and a discriminating artistic taste.

This character sketch would be incomplete without noting that he was an extraordinarily supernatural person. Mgr. Escrivá loved God and the Church in a quite remarkable way. He had the gift of drawing souls to God. In 1941, in a letter to the abbot of Montserrat to refute slander being spread about Fr. Escrivá at the time, the bishop of Madrid, who knew the founder well and who had encouraged him from the very beginning, described him as 'a model priest, chosen by God for the sanctification of many souls, humble, prudent, full of abnegation, extremely docile toward his prelate, remarkably intelligent with a very solid doctrinal and spiritual formation, ardently zealous, and an apostle for the Christian formation of youth'.

CONTINUITY

His successor

At the time of Mgr. Escrivá's death Opus Dei was in all five continents and comprised some 60,000 members of 80 nationalities.

Observers have been struck by the fact that the sudden death of the founder caused no upheaval of any kind: this continuity indicates the members' faithfulness to the spirit of the Work and to the legacy of its founder. Three months after his death, on 15 September 1975, 172 representatives of all the members gathered together in an elective congress to choose a successor. The vote was unanimous, on the first ballot, electing Fr. Alvaro del Portillo, who for forty years had been the founder's closest aide. When Opus Dei was made a personal prelature in 1982, Pope

John Paul II appointed Fr. del Portillo its first prelate. Fr. del Portillo was born on 11 March 1914 in Madrid. His first qualification was in civil engineering, and he also held doctorates in history and canon law. He had been a member of Opus Dei since 1935 and was one of the first three members of Opus Dei ordained in 1944.

In addition to his priestly work and his duties as Secretary General of Opus Dei, Mgr. del Portillo took an active part in the Second Vatican Council, notably as president of the preparatory Commission for the laity and as secretary to the Commission for the discipline of the clergy. He acted as a consultor to several congregations of the Roman Curia. He was Chancellor of the universities of Navarre (Spain), of Piura (Peru) and of La Sabana (Colombia). Two of his books have been published in English: *Faithful and Laity in the Church* (Ecclesia Press, Shannon 1972), and *On Priesthood* (Scepter, New York 1974).

The expansion of Opus Dei

This takes place when apostolic works begin in new countries, and through the extension of activities in places where Opus Dei is already established.

What happens seems to be the same everywhere: when members find work in a place where the message of the Work is as yet unknown, they begin their personal apostolate, making friends and organising formation talks in their homes. Vocations arise and a small nucleus is built up little by little. A priest of Opus Dei visits them regularly, with the approval of the local bishop. Soon it becomes necessary to find temporary premises, and eventually a recognised centre is established. In this way they are putting into practice the advice of the Founder: 'You need to spread out, throughout the whole world, among all honest occupations of men, each of you bringing ten or so friends attached, as it were, to his fingers, and they in their turn bringing more friends . . . You have to open out like a fan.'

The number of vocations has continued to grow. In 1984, nine years after the death of the founder, Opus Dei had more than 74,000 members of 87 nationalities. Between 1975 and 1984, moreover, apostolic work has begun in Bolivia, Honduras, Trinidad, Ivory Coast, Zaire, Taiwan, Hong Kong, Singapore and Sweden.

Its founder saw Opus Dei continuing 'for as long as there are men on earth. No matter how much production techniques may change there will always be work which men can offer up to God and sanctify in his presence.' Thus Opus Dei will always have its reason for being.

In fact Mgr. Escrivá often used to say: 'We are not an organisation which has arisen because of some particular set of circumstances; we have not come to meet the needs of a specific country or of a specific period in history; from the very beginning Jesus wanted his work to have a universal and catholic heart.'

Opus Dei in Ireland

In Ireland, members are to be found all over the country, from Donegal to Cork, from Galway to Dublin. Most live in areas where centres of the Prelature have been set up: Dublin, Galway, Tuam, Meath and Limerick.

One of the first apostolic initiatives of members in Ireland was the establishment of Nullamore University Residence in Dartry, Dublin. The official opening in 1954 was attended by the Taoiseach, Mr John A. Costello; the Chancellor of the National University of Ireland and leader of Fianna Fáil, Mr Eamon de Valera; the President of University College Dublin, Professor Michael Tierney, and the Registrar, Professor Jeremiah Hogan; the Lord Mayor, Mr Alfie Byrne; and the Archbishop of Dublin, Dr John Charles McQuaid. Later years saw the expansion of Nullamore, which now houses 60 students from Ireland and abroad.

Further halls of residence were set up in the years that followed: Gort Ard (Salthill, Galway) in 1958; Glenard (Clonskeagh, Dublin) in 1962; Ros Geal (University Road,

Galway) in 1972. Activities for students in Dublin are also held in study centres such as Cleraun (Mount Merrion), Carraigburn (Donnybrook) and Ely (Hume Street).

Over the years, members have also set up a variety of youth clubs. These include the Helm Club (Galway), the Harrow Canoe Club (Ranelagh, Dublin), Dunevin (Synge Street, Dublin), Glenbeag (Clonskeagh), Nullamore Junior Club (Dartry, Dublin) and the Anchor Youth Club in Artane on Dublin's Northside. These offer a wide range of activities for young people.

Catering and Educational Centres such as Crannton (Dartry, Dublin), Ballabbert (Tuam) and Lisdara (Navan) offer a two year course in catering and household administration leading to a City and Guilds qualification.

A variety of courses, including retreats, for members and others, are organised regularly throughout the year in two Conference Centres: Lismullin, at Tara, Co. Meath and Ballyglunin, near Tuam, Co. Galway.

In Ireland as elsewhere, the apostolic activity of members can be found in all sectors of society: among blue and white collar workers, academics and tradesmen, those working inside and outside the home, and among the young and old.

Opus Dei in Britain

As in Ireland, members of the Work live in all parts of the country, but mainly in places where centres have been set up, with the previous agreement of the Ordinary of the diocese: Glasgow, Manchester, London (where the Work has developed most, with 12 centres in all), and Oxford. Activities are also organised in Canterbury, Mansfield, Portsmouth, Southend, in mid-Sussex and on Merseyside, although permanent centres have not yet been established in these places.

Some corporate apostolic activities have been started, such as Netherhall House, an international university student residence for men in London; Lakefield Catering and Educational Centre, also in London, a school for training girls of school-leaving age in domestic and catering skills; and various residences for university students and clubs for young people throughout the country. These centres not only reach out to academic environments, but also extend to non-intellectual spheres, attracting employers as well as employees, appealing to the young as well as to older people.

Reputation for sanctity

Even during his lifetime Mgr. Escrivá had a reputation for holiness, which might be summed up in a private comment made by Paul VI. The Pope, who had known him since 1946, considered him to be, in the history of the Church, 'the person who has received most charisms and has responded to these gifts with greatest generosity'.

This reputation for holiness, 'supported by numerous and authorised witnesses' has gone on increasing since 1975 'with remarkable spontaneity', as Cardinal Poletti wrote in the decree by which, less than six years after Mgr. Escrivá's death 'in an odour of sanctity', he opened his process of beatification in Rome. Many thousands of letters requesting this decision were received by the Pope: from heads of state, government ministers and members of parliament, from entire families, from people and institutions of every type and from the four corners of the globe; requests also came from 69 cardinals and 1300 bishops, that is to say from a third of the entire hierarchy of the church – something quite unique.

Favours attributed to Josemaría Escrivá continue to reach the Roman office of his cause of canonisation. They come from every country and include regions of the world where Opus Dei is not yet established. They involve material favours, including inexplicable medical cures well supported by medical evidence. But the most common favours are of a spiritual kind, and most of them will never be recorded. A certain glimpse of these is given in the Newsletter distributed free of charge by the office for the Causes of Saints of the Opus Dei Prelature in each country (In Britain:

4 Orme Court, London W2 4RL, in Ireland: Harvieston, Cunningham Road, Dalkey, Co. Dublin). His influence is also felt through his writings. More than 7 million copies of his books are in print.

On 17 May 1992, Pope John Paul II beatified Josemaría Escrivá in St Peter's Square before a crowd of some 300,000 people, including 33 cardinals and over 200 bishops from all over the world. In his homily, the Pope said: 'With supernatural intuition Blessed Josemaría untiringly preached the universal call to holiness and apostolate. Christ calls everyone to become holy in the realities of everyday life. Hence, *work too is a means of personal holiness and apostolate*, when it is done in union with Jesus Christ ... In a society in which an unbridled craving for material things turns them into idols and a cause of separation from God, the new *Beatus* reminds us that these same realities, creatures of God and of human industry, if used correctly for the glory of the Creator and the service of one's brothers and sisters, *can be a way for men and women to meet Christ.*'

Other members of Opus Dei are also being considered for beatification. These include Isidoro Zorzano (1902–1943), a railway engineer, one of the first members of Opus Dei; Monserrat Grases (1942–1959), a young Catalan girl who died of bone cancer at age 17; Guadalupe Ortiz (1916–1975), who helped to start the women's apostolates of Opus Dei in Mexico, and her brother Eduardo Ortiz (1910–1985), a doctor of medicine, married with seven children; Tony Zweifel (1938–1989), a professional engineer from Switzerland; and Bishop Alvaro del Portillo (1914–1994), one of the first three Opus Dei priests, who in 1975 succeeded Blessed Josemaría at the head of Opus Dei.

2: The Spirituality of Opus Dei

On 2 October 1928 Fr. Escrivá de Balaguer knew the full import of what God wanted of him. He saw Opus Dei clearly defined in its basic outlines. The insight he received was not a general inspiration, but a precise, definite illumination; his work was to be 'not a human undertaking, but a great supernatural undertaking, that from the beginning has seen fulfilled to the letter everything necessary for it to be called, without presumption, the "Work of God".'

Even at the very beginning he was able to describe it all in detail to those he confided in: it was as if he were speaking of something already established. In his first writings he reveals its newness: everyone is called to holiness and to apostolate, without leaving the world, by elevating to a supernatural plane the temporal realities in which he or she is immersed, particularly his or her everyday work, family responsibilities and social duties. This idea seems obvious enough now, but it was not so back in 1928. To show how new it was we need to put it in the context of the history of spirituality.

A call to seek holiness in the world, in one's job, makes no sense if one is not convinced that 'worldly' things can be sanctified, and can sanctify the person engaged in them. But the whole panorama changes once one does perceive the Christian meaning of worldly realities, and then commits oneself, as the founder urged, to sanctify them, with a sense of having received a divine vocation to do precisely this. The important thing to notice is that Mgr. Escrivá was not content with proclaiming the doctrine of sanctification in the midst of the world in an abstract way, as a theory. He encouraged specific individuals to search for holiness and to carry out apostolate in and through their secular duties. A truly pastoral phenomenon began to take shape 'fostered in our time by divine Providence, for the good of the church and of all

25

souls, with the abundant blessings of five popes' (Mgr. Carboni, at the inauguration ceremony of the Opus Dei Prelature).

HISTORICAL BACKGROUND

The religious concept

Very early in the life of Christianity, work had ceased to be regarded as something good in itself; rather it came to be seen mainly as an ascetical means to avoid idleness, the mother of all vices. This is the opinion of Saint Athanasius and Cassian.

Cenobitic life (apart from the world and monastic in style) grew in importance, although Saint John Chrysostom in particular still paid much attention to work. But of the more prominent Fathers of the Church, he was actually the last to speak of the sanctification of ordinary life in the same terms as Vatican II was to use centuries later. After him, one has the impression that the average Christian was not considered to be called to live the Gospel fully. This was the situation up to the fifth century.

Nor does apostolate seem to have been considered an obligation for the individual Christian. In the rule of Saint Benedict, it is the monastery, rather than the monk, that does the apostolate.

The appearance of the mendicant orders brought an emphasis on preaching, with the friars travelling from town to town. This does not really point to an affirmation of the value of ordinary work: rather the opposite. To be sure, manual work carried out in the monastery did have a certain material resemblance to work carried out in the world. Theoretically it was possible to strive to sanctify this work. However, the argument between the mendicant orders and the secular clergy in the thirteenth century led the former to insist on the possibility of sanctifying oneself without work, and of maintaining oneself by alms alone.

The theologians of the mendicant orders did not in fact explore what work really means. They argued that manual work was not obligatory. Even Saint Thomas Aquinas saw secular occupations as an obstacle to contemplation. Saint Bonaventure and many others were of the same opinion.

Other institutions more directly present in the world (military orders and mediaeval guilds for example) provided scarcely any ascetical or doctrinal formation that might favour an awareness of the need to sanctify work.

In the following centuries attention was directed away from work. The author of *The Imitation of Christ* had an even more negative outlook on work than the desert fathers. For subsequent spiritual writers 'work' was reduced to mean the effort involved in asceticism (the spiritual struggle to be perfect). This was the concept of Cisneros in his *Exercitatorio* and of St Ignatius of Loyola in his *Spiritual Exercises*, which is largely inspired by the former.

The Renaissance brought a positive development of a kind: one has only to think of such men as St Thomas More or Erasmus. But it was a long, slow process. Luther's split from Rome in the sixteenth century, giving birth to Protestantism, postponed the discovery of the sanctifying value of work. Indeed, the Protestant concept of original sin as radically corruptive of human nature, and its view that human actions had no redemptive value – even those performed in a state of grace – was totally opposed to such a discovery.

The other great upheaval of the sixteenth century, the discovery of unevangelised peoples, might conceivably have favoured a drawing together of the priesthood, and the life of perfection, and a more effective apostolate, better adapted to the needs of the times.

Renaissance and Baroque Catholic theology, however, allowed itself to be contaminated by the ideas of an aristocracy that looked down on manual work, and by a narrow, uninspiring moralism. The new theology was also suspicious of certain excesses, particularly in the realm of mysticism. With Melchor Cano, it declared that lay people could not aspire to the peaks of Christian perfection. Suarez, the distinguished Jesuit theologian, put forward the theory of the 'states', according to which religious and bishops –

and by analogy, priests – are by their vocation in an 'acquired state of perfection' which they then communicate to others. The ordinary Christian was seen as powerless to reach any significant degree of perfection, a theory which subsequently rigidly constrained ways of thinking about the call to holiness.

In the seventeenth century there was a reaction, evidenced in the aspirations of prominent but ordinary Christians to follow the pathways of prayer. The most notable representative of this tendency was St Francis de Sales. Generally speaking, however, he went no further than to suggest that lay people use the means to sanctity used by religious, adapting them where necessary to suit their circumstances.

Nevertheless, since secular activity was not seen as leading naturally or easily to sanctity, spiritual writing soon put forward church-related activity as the foundation of human work.

After the French Revolution, religious spirituality began to evolve towards a presence in the world, and attention was given to earthly activities as opposed to purely physical work. Nevertheless, material distancing from the world remained a basic attitude. It was a question of living 'like' others, of 'approaching' the world, of 'drawing near to', of 'joining' those who work, and so on. And the religious associations that went on being formed continued to have the centre of their spiritual life outside the world. Moreover, apostolate was seen as something external, superimposed on presence in the world.

The net effects of these trends was that, at the time Opus Dei started, spiritually conscious lay people were torn between their desire to sanctify themselves (which seemed to imply withdrawal from the world) and their concern to remain in the world (to which they were closely tied by their family and professional involvements).

Some embraced a life of devotion and charitable works, trying to achieve 'as best they could' the religious state in a life of evangelical perfection. There were three consequences of this: (a) the desire for holiness meant having to procure moments for recollection *apart from* one's daily occupation; (b) it still implied a concept of lay holiness radically inferior to the superior holiness of the religious; and (c) as, according to St Thomas, the virtue of religion is a *natural* virtue only, a spirituality of this nature does not readily insert the lay person as such into the *supernatural* life. As he strives to 'accumulate' religious, virtuous and charitable acts, turning his back on his everyday duties, the 'devout' layman must frequently see his work and the duties of his state in life as obstacles to his sanctification.

For others, the holiness of lay people took on an essentially moral character. That is, everything had to be filled with goodness: to be a good father, carry out one's family duties well, work diligently, be well-behaved, and so on. But this has also meant staying on the natural plane, with the real risk of degenerating towards being a mere 'do-gooder', satisfied with being blameless, but not at all concerned with the call to holiness.

Opus Dei

The renewal in the evolution of the religious state and the birth of Opus Dei more or less coincide in time. But there the resemblance ends. 'I consider the path of the religious vocation to be blessed and necessary for the Church,' Mgr. Escrivá declared. 'But it is not my path, nor even that of the members of the Work. One can even say that on coming to the Work, each and every person does so on the explicit condition of not changing his state' (i.e. remaining in the 'secular' state, not changing to the 'religious' state).

These two approaches to holiness are movements in opposite directions. The evolution of the religious state is a movement beginning from outside the world, but going towards it, seeking a presence there. The secular spirituality of Opus Dei on the other hand has its being in the world; it begins in the world, and sets out to make it holy from within, to lead it to God. It brings together Christians of all types, who, in the words of Mgr. Escrivá 'being in the world, or rather being of the world, since they are ordinary lay people, aspire to Christian perfection by reason of a divine vocation. Our vocation means that our secular condition, our ordinary work, our situation in the world, is our only path to holiness and apostolate. It is not a matter of using a secular occupation as a cover for our apostolic work. On the contrary, our occupation is the same one we would have had if we had not come to Opus Dei; the same one we would have if we were unfortunate enough to abandon our vocation. We are, my sons and daughters, ordinary people. When we work in temporal affairs, we do so because that is our place, that is where we encounter Jesus Christ, that is where our vocation leaves us.'

This is what led Cardinal Luciani, the future Pope John Paul I, to say that where St Francis de Sales proposed a spirituality for lay people, Mgr. Escrivá offers a lay spirituality, a secular spirituality. The pastoral phenomenon of Opus Dei 'does not arise out of opposition to religious spiritualities; it is a distinct outpouring of the perennial treasure of the Gospel'; it was born 'from below', from ordinary life, and 'is not', according to its founder, 'a kind of compromise with the world – a "desacralization" of the monastic or religious life. It is not the latest stage in the rapprochement of the religious and the world'.

The message of Opus Dei, is therefore something 'as old as the Gospel and as new as the Gospel', reaching back over the centuries to the first Christians, who normally lived and worked in the midst of society.

THE SANCTIFICATION OF WORK

Basic principles

A text of the founder reveals the full scope of the kind of sanctification he preached: 'Anyone who thought that our supernatural life is built up by turning our back on work would not understand our vocation. For us, in fact, work is a specific means to sanctity. Our interior life – as contemplatives in the midst of the world –

takes its origin and its impulse from the external life of work of each of us. We cannot separate our interior life from our apostolic work: it is all one. External work should not cause any interruption in prayer, just as the beating of our heart does not interrupt the attention we give to our activities, whatever they may be.'

Mgr. Escrivá shows what Genesis (2:15) means when it says that man has been created to work – 'ut operaretur'. If that is the human condition, then ordinary work is the very hinge of man's sanctification and the right human and supernatural environment for him to help his fellow men.

The fact that this statement in Genesis about work comes before the original sin of our first parents, shows that work is of the very essence of human nature. Only the laborious and tedious side of human activity is the punishment of original sin. Work in itself is good, is noble. Man is wholly fulfilled by his work, by being conscious of what he does. That is precisely what constitutes his superiority over other created things.

Work, taken in its widest sense, is part of God's plan for mankind. It is 'a means by which man shares in creation. Hence work, any kind of work, is not only worthy; it is also a means of attaining human – that is, earthly, natural – perfection, as well as supernatural perfection.'

Man is a co-creator as well as a co-redeemer with God. Christ worked; St Joseph taught him his carpenter's trade; work therefore is something which in turn has been redeemed. It is not just the framework of human life; it is a path to sanctity, something that sanctifies and that can be sanctified. For man-in-the-world work becomes the hinge on which the whole task of sanctification turns.

This is what led the founder of Opus Dei to sum up life on earth by saying that one must 'sanctify work, sanctify oneself in one's work and sanctify others [other persons and things] through one's work.' The three things are interconnected: personal sanctity ('sanctify oneself in one's work') and apostolate ('sanctify through work') are not things one can achieve just by 'using'

31

work, or operating in a working context, as though work were juxtaposed with them and separable from them. Sanctity and apostolate are achieved *through working*, while the same work constitutes a central part of man's very existence and so itself needs to be sanctified.

Sanctification of work

The first element of this trio is the sanctification of work carried out in the world. The world in itself is good, because it has come from God's hands. The hatred, pride, violence, rivalries, and so on, to be found in it, are the result of the original sin of Adam and Eve and of the personal sins of individual men and women. These sins corrupt the world and turn it away from God.

As regards the world, the spirit of Opus Dei is optimistic: the Christian has the mission of restoring it to its original goodness by leading it back to God and making of it an occasion of holiness. Instead of the 'contempt of the world' and 'leaving the world' characteristic of the religious vocation, Mgr. Escrivá preached love of the world 'because it is where we live, because it is our battlefield – a splendid battle of love and peace – and because it is there that we must sanctify ourselves and sanctify others'. He saw the whole of creation as needing to be led back to God; just as King Midas transformed all he touched into gold, human work needs to become 'through love, the Work of God, Opus Dei, *operatio Dei*, a supernatural work'.

Once this principle is established, it follows that all noble occupations, especially work, can and must be sanctified. In so far as work is a sharing in the creative activity of God, the Christian must carry it out with a supernatural outlook. No work is to be rejected. All employments are of value in God's service. All of them are of the greatest importance, because in the end 'their value depends on the love of God with which they are carried out'. Mgr. Escrivá rebelled against any attempt to classify people according to their occupation, as though some jobs were nobler than others. He declared, 'What does it matter to me if he be a cabinet minister or a road sweeper? What I care about is that he sanctify himself in his work.'

Such a concept of work allows one to aim at 'placing Christ at the summit of all human activities', that is, to lead them all to their fulness and draw from them all the spiritual consequences. This implies two things for the Christian.

First, that he should carry out his work with all the perfection of which he is capable, from both the natural and the supernatural points of view. For work to be sanctified the worker must do it with a right intention, supernaturally. Mgr. Escrivá sums it up like this: 'Add a supernatural motive to your daily work and you will have sanctified it.' In addition, one must sanctify one's work by using the insight of faith to discover its ultimate purpose – the absolute good, God – and by learning to carry it out with charity and hope. This supernatural 'ultimate purpose' is part of the plan of redemption; it incorporates and elevates all the intermediate purposes of man (natural ends and the plan of creation), raising them to the order of grace. An essential part of the sanctification of ordinary work consists in 'doing work well, with human perfection also, and fulfilling all professional and social obligations well'.

And secondly, the Christian is led to evaluate his environment to see how he can contribute to 'restoring to the world the divine goodness of its true order', and to exerting a good influence on it in accordance with the social doctrine of the Church. Through work man leaves his stamp on creation. Work enables him to support his family, to contribute to the improvement of society, and to the progress of all mankind, by developing ways of life, of coexistence and fraternity that help make his fellow men more human and so more open to receiving the supernatural message of salvation.

Sanctifying oneself in one's work

The second aspect of the spirituality of work as conceived by Mgr. Escrivá has to do with personal sanctification through work:

'What use is it telling me that so-and-so is a good son of mine – a good Christian – but a bad shoemaker? If he doesn't try to learn his trade well, or doesn't give his full attention to it, he won't be able to sanctify it or offer it to our Lord. The sanctification of ordinary work is, as it were, the hinge of true spirituality.'

Work becomes the prime place where almost all virtues are brought into play. Indeed, work done in the presence of God is a continuous prayer, since it involves the theological virtues that are the peak of Christian life namely charity, faith and hope.

(a) First, it involves practising *charity*, 'by striving to seal all one's actions with the love of God, generously serving one's fellow men, all souls.' The man who does his job conscientiously renders a direct service to society, takes weight off others, and helps provide assistance for less privileged individuals or countries. The problems of mankind cannot be solved by justice alone. Charity is also needed, as in the time of the Apostles; they opened up a pathway in the corrupt pagan world of their day by means of this supernatural virtue; charity is 'a generous overflow of justice', and God has ordained that the first requirement of justice is to do one's duty. 'The way to start is by being just; the next step is to do what is most equitable . . .' To do this means working for others. God puts a choice before us: either to work selfishly, for ourselves, or to dedicate ourselves fully to the service of others.

(b) *Faith* is also present in work. On the one hand, Mgr. Escrivá is convinced that a person's normal occupation, however ordinary and commonplace it might seem, has great value in the eyes of God and has its place in the plan of salvation. On the other hand, for him, the presence of Christ in the centre of the soul activates one's faith, and is a constant stimulus to contemplation. 'Our life is work and prayer, and, the other way round, prayer and work. The moment comes when we can no longer separate these two concepts, these two words, contemplation and action, which end up meaning the same thing in our mind and in our soul.' If the ordinary Christian does not work, if he does not carry out his obligations, he can have no life of prayer, no contemplative life. Without contemplative life there is no point in wanting to work for Christ.

(c) In the third place *hope* comes into play: one hopes to be able to sanctify oneself through one's work and to obtain from God the reward that this work deserves, for no sincere effort is in vain. One must also have the *fortitude* to persevere day after day, however difficult things become, whatever the external circumstances, until the task is completed, overcoming setbacks and the occasional lack of resources, trying always to be an example. One also requires *prudence*, which enables one to see what must be done in each situation and how to set about doing it. Work also develops other social virtues such as loyalty, faithfulness to commitments and to ties of friendship; overcoming restraints of work, etc.; and naturalness, which avoids anything strange, anything that does not fit in with one's position. This naturalness is a sign of the human and spiritual maturity of a person who fully accepts his responsibilities; it also shows his humility in not seeking personal satisfaction, but the will of God alone. ('When you hear the applause of triumph, let there also sound in your ears the laughter you provoke by your failures.')

So in the eyes of Mgr. Escrivá, 'ordinary life is not without its value. If the fact of doing the same things day after day seems boring, dull, monotonous, it is because there is not enough love there. When love is present, every new day has a different colour, a different rhythm, a different harmony.'

Holiness cannot therefore be reserved to a few privileged souls – those who have been ordained to the priesthood, or whose religious vocation sets them apart from the world. The message of the founder of Opus Dei was much more optimistic and open. When it was first proclaimed it was revolutionary: all men and all women of every social background, every race, culture, language, and professional situation, young and old, married, widowed or single, ill or healthy, priests and lay people, can and should seek holiness, as the Second Vatican Council was to declare thirty-five years later.

Holiness is one and the same for all: it means progressive

identification with God, in whose image and likeness man has been created. Each person must seek holiness in his own particular situation – professional work, family life, social relationships, leisure, and so on.

Sanctifying others through work

One's vocation to work in some profession or trade cannot be cut off from one's condition as a Christian, but should be a 'lamp that gives light' to colleagues and friends. The sanctification of temporal structures is, in Mgr. Escrivá's view, an aspect of apostolate that is inseparable from apostolic action with individual persons. Each person's occupation and social situation creates a series of links with colleagues, as well as other professional, family and social connections. This is usually how family and social relationships are built up. Sincere, true, disinterested friendship leads to the greatest good – God himself. As a result of this friendship, based on sacrifice, trust is born spontaneously. The heart of a friend is attentive to all one's problems, desires and feelings: 'Those well-timed words, whispered in the ear of your wavering friend, the helpful conversation that you managed to start at the right moment; the ready professional advice that improves his university work; the discreet indiscretion by which you open up unsuspected horizons for his zeal. This all forms part of the "apostolate of friendship".'

In the words of the founder, Opus Dei is 'a great work of catechesis', that fights ignorance – 'God's greatest enemy' – through the apostolate of example and doctrine. This apostolic activity is in the main the work of individuals, who carry it out in their work situations, with their colleagues, creating in a natural way opportunities to talk about God, about supernatural topics, and about the sort of approach a Christian must have in all the different situations that ordinary life throws up. Speaking from experience, the founder would exhort his audience: 'Work at your job, trying to fulfil the duties of your state in life, doing your job, your everyday work, properly, improving at it, getting better each day. Be loyal; be understanding with others and demanding on yourself. Be mortified and cheerful. This will be your apostolate. Then though you won't see why, because you're very aware of your own wretchedness, you will find that people come to you. Then you can talk to them, quite simply and naturally on your way home from work, for instance, or in a family gathering, on a bus, walking down the street, anywhere. You will chat about the sort of longings that everyone feels deep down in his soul, even though some may not want to notice them: they will come to understand them better, and then begin to look for God in earnest.

This is the service that the Catholic Church expects from the members of Opus Dei, as set out in the solemn decree of approval of Opus Dei, *Primum inter* (16 June 1950); a service offered 'through the example they give to their fellow citizens, their colleagues and workmates, in family, civil and professional life, by striving always and everywhere to be the best'.

Work well done gives good example. The Christian must bring to it all the perfection he or she is capable of on the human or natural level (professional competence), and on the divine level (for love of God and as a service to souls), so that by objective standards his or her work is seen to be well done. It is difficult for work to be sanctified unless the worker tries to do it perfectly. Without that perfection it will be almost impossible to acquire the necessary prestige, described by Mgr. Escrivá as that 'professorship from which you will teach others to sanctify their work and adapt their lives to the demands of the Christian faith'. Hence the need for on-going professional training to acquire all the natural knowledge one can. To win over others, a person must take to heart his need to carry out his duties as well as the best of his companions, and if possible, better than the best.

Obviously, therefore, apostolate is not just some pious exercises that have no connection with what takes up the greater part of one's time. 'The apostolic concern which burns in the heart of ordinary Christians' is intimately bound up with everyday work.

FREEDOM AND RESPONSIBILITY

The concept of freedom

One of the characteristics of the spirit of Opus Dei frequently pointed out by its spokesmen is the high regard it has for freedom. This love of freedom is closely connected with Opus Dei's inherently secular outlook. It means that in all professional, political, social and similar maters, each member acts according to the dictates of a well-formed conscience and accepts responsibility for all consequences of his decisions and actions. He learns not only to respect but positively to love and promote true pluralism, the variety of everything human: in the words of the Declaration of the Sacred Congregation for Bishops of 23 August 1982, 'as regards choice in professional, social, political matters, etc., the lay faithful belonging to the Prelature enjoy, within the limits of Catholic faith and morals the Church discipline, the same freedom as other Catholics, their fellow-citizens; as a result the Prelature is not responsible for the professional, social, political or economic activities of any of its members'.

This disposition of Opus Dei in favour of freedom is not a matter of tactics or shrewdness; it is the logical consequence of the awareness by members of Opus Dei that they are in the one mission of the Church, the salvation of souls.

It is true that the Christian spirit lays down certain general ethical principles for temporal action – respect and support of the Magisterium of the Church; noble and loyal behaviour, fostering charity; understanding and respect for the opinions of others; true love of one's country, free from narrow nationalism; promotion of justice, readiness to make sacrifices in serving the interests of the civic community, etc. However, on the basis of these principles each person chooses, from among the different possible solutions or options open to him, whatever he thinks best. Mgr. Escrivá concludes: 'With our blessed freedom Opus Dei can never be, in the political life of a country, a kind of political party: there is and always will be room within Opus Dei for all outlooks and approaches allowed by a Christian conscience, and it is impossible for the directors to bring any influence to bear.' Only the hierarchy of the church has the authority, if it considers it necessary for the welfare of souls, to establish a specific norm of behaviour for all Catholics.

This programme of personal holiness and apostolate in ordinary life, particularly in the sphere of everyday work, cannot be successful without the freedom that is the birthright of men and women created in the image of God. Personal freedom is essential in Christian life, especially when each person assumes full responsibility for his own affairs.

Christianity is of its nature a religion of freedom. This was self-evident for the founder of Opus Dei. 'God wants us to serve him freely – "ubi autem Spiritus Domini, ibi libertas" (2 Cor 3:17), where the Lord's spirit is, there is freedom – and therefore an apostolate which did not respect freedom of consciences would certainly be wrong.' Nowadays some people fear that the promotion of freedom may endanger the faith. That would indeed be the case if the freedom in question were an aimless freedom, one that was lawless and irresponsible. Rather than freedom that would be licence; it would amount to saying that anything pleasing, anything one felt like doing, was morally good even if it involved rejecting God. This is the end-result of what is called 'freedom of conscience', which is not the same thing at all as 'freedom of consciences'. With Leo XIII, Mgr. Escrivá declared: 'I defend with all my strength the freedom of consciences, which means that no one may licitly prevent a person from worshipping God.' While man has a serious obligation to search for truth, no one may compel him to practise a faith he has not received; nor compel him to profess it in a particular way where God himself has left each Christian free to decide; nor, when he has received it from God, impose restrictions on its practice.

Criticism of Opus Dei

The total respect for freedom as practised by Mgr. Escrivá from the very beginning of Opus Dei was not always well understood. Perhaps the Spain of the 40s and 50s was not ready for it, particularly in clerical circles.

Certain spiritual trends of the time, deriving from various theological schools, ascetical approaches and apostolic points of view, had created deep divisions among the laity and led to a certain 'messianic' tendency (each little group claiming it had '*the* solution' to all the world's problems), that Mgr. Escrivá called 'the pseudo-spiritual one-party mentality', everyone thinking that his principles and his attitudes were the only valid ones and that everyone else should take them on board. It was only a short step – easily taken – to regarding the views of others as pernicious or heretical.

Thus the opposition that arose from 1929 on (See *Conversations with Mgr. Escrivá de Balaguer*, Four Courts Press, Dublin, 1980 edition, nos. 33 & 64–66.) can be explained by a lack of understanding of the basic message of Opus Dei: nobody believed that it was possible to aspire to sanctity while remaining in the world. The year 1939 saw an increase in criticism and persecution of Opus Dei by 'good people', who – as the founder said while he forgave them – 'did so much evil whilst perhaps thinking that they were serving God'.

These attacks took place at times in the confessional or from the professorial chair. Sometimes they appeared in the press or when these good people visited the families of members of Opus Dei. Endless anxiety was caused when parents were told that their children 'were in danger of hell' because they had been 'led to believe' that one could be holy in the midst of the world. Students were sent to spy on the centres of Opus Dei and to denounce the heresies and deviations that took place there. One day Fr. Escrivá's first book, *The Way*, was publicly burned in a convent school in Barcelona, where the provincial governor had issued a warrant for the arrest of its author. The founder had also been denounced before the post Civil War military tribunal for the suppression of freemasonry. Opus Dei was described as the 'Jewish branch of freemasonry' or 'a Jewish sect connected with freemasonry'. Later Mgr. Escrivá was accused before the Holy Office, now the Congregation for the Doctrine of the Faith, after the Holy See had granted Opus Dei its definitive approval.

The founder suffered because of these obstacles placed in his way, above all because of the harm caused to souls, not least the souls of the 'good people' instigating the attacks. In spite of everything he never lost his serenity: he was not particularly surprised by this development. 'A picture that was all light and no shade . . . would not be a picture! . . . So, misunderstandings and opposition have their usefulness'.

It is this clash between two outlooks – one religious, the other lay – which should complement each other and not be antagonistic, that caused certain misunderstandings, certain campaigns against Opus Dei. They spread from some ecclesiastical circles to circles that are not normally well-disposed towards the Church, and they still appear from time to time.

Freedom and work

The freedom of members of Opus Dei is seen first of all in their everyday work – in their choice of work, and then in their choice of the means to do it as well as they can. Members are accountable only to whoever is above them at work, for example, the owner of the company, or government department if they are civil servants, but never to the directors of Opus Dei.

If Opus Dei does not interfere in their work, still less does it make use of its members' professional influence to obtain privileges or preferment. This would go completely against the purely spiritual nature of the institution. One could even say that such an attempt would be contrary to what one has the right to expect of any honest person, Christian or not. Mgr. Escrivá said quite clearly: 'Opus Dei is an apostolic undertaking. It is interested only in souls. Our morality does not permit us to behave like a self-help or mutual-support society.'

The only influence Opus Dei has on the work of its members is through the spiritual training it gives them, which motivates them to become increasingly aware of the implications of the Gospel message and to strive to apply it to their daily lives.

Hence there is a sensitivity to questions of social justice, at the same time leaving the door open to a possible variety of solutions. For the founder, 'the Catholic solution' to the many problems facing the world does not exist. Any solution will be Christian if it respects natural law and the Gospel teaching. He therefore stressed not the material aspect of the solution but the spirit that should inspire it.

With this emphasis, he energetically encouraged each individual to accept his responsibilities, because one cannot 'remain passive when confronted with all the injustice, social and personal, which the human heart can cause'. Mgr. Escrivá denounced a situation so often found in society: 'so many centuries of people living side by side and still so much hatred, so much destruction, so much fanaticism stored up in eyes that do not want to see and in hearts that do not want to love! The good things of the earth monopolized by a handful of people; the culture of the world confined to cliques. And, on the outside, hunger for bread and education. Human lives – holy, because they come from God – treated as mere things, as statistics.'

A businessman, for example, motivated by this concern, will be opposed to unfair competition, fraud, or price rises due only to a monopoly; he will favour honesty in commercial dealings; he will pay special attention to the problems and living conditions of his employees; he will practise the virtue of justice in his relations with his workers, and so on. In turn a workman will strive to fulfil all his duties faithfully; and all citizens will exercise their rights and fulfil their obligations bearing in mind the good of others and of the country.

This influence of the spirit of Opus Dei on society is far from insignificant. But in the last analysis it comes back to whatever personal influence individual members may acquire through their professional prestige and their standing in their particular sphere of activity.

A desire to contribute to the solution of social problems – and here the Christian has so much to offer – leads members of Opus Dei to combine with others to develop works of apostolate which have considerable social impact.

In reply to certain orchestrated criticism, Mgr. Escrivá commented that it would be absurd to think that Opus Dei as such could manage mines, banks, or any other commercial enterprise. To illustrate his statement let us imagine a large family. A son works at the Central Bank, a daughter at the head office of IBM, another is on the staff of Marks and Spencer, and so on. Does this make the modest family the owner or controller of these great businesses? The same can be said of Opus Dei.

The founder realised that a partisan minority will never understand the practical implications of freedom and that they 'would like us to explain things in their way – in terms of a power struggle and pressure groups. If they are not given an explanation along these lines (in other words a false one, in keeping with their warped outlook) they continue to allege deception and sinister intrigue'.

The members of Opus Dei reject such insinuations. For them it is unthinkable that they should use their membership of the Prelature for personal ends, professional success, 'jobs for the boys', or to climb the social ladder, or as a means of imposing opinions on others. The other members would not tolerate this and would ask any one who tried it 'to change his attitude or leave the Work. This is a point on which no one in Opus Dei can ever permit the least deviation. It is their duty to defend not only their own personal freedom but also the supernatural character of the activity to which they have dedicated their lives. That is why I think that personal freedom and responsibility are the best guarantee of the supernatural purpose of the Work of God.'

If some members of Opus Dei occupy important positions or have high social standing, it is due to their own personal efforts to sanctify their work, and never to pressure from Opus Dei or favouritism from other members. Each member knows he is completely free, not only in making up his mind on issues, but also in his professional activities – in choosing his job, appointing others to jobs, managing his business, etc. And all of them strive to act within the moral principles that apply when appointing or employing others, while taking into account individual merit and the public good. Justice alone would demand as much.

Freedom and politics

Those who do not accept that religious ideals or moral values can bring people together in a common undertaking, which transcends political differences, might consider a purely sociological point. Members of Opus Dei belong to 87 nationalities and all social classes, races and cultures, throughout the five continents. Each of them lives with his family and works in his own work environment. How could the institution impose on such heterogeneous and widely dispersed individuals one political criterion, a kind of dogma, in a subject as relative and debatable as politics? How could a Kenyan be asked to model his behaviour on that of an Australian, a citizen of Guatemala on that of a citizen of the Philippines, an inhabitant of Singapore on that of someone from Luxemburg? Indeed, Mgr. Escrivá repeatedly stressed that by its very nature 'Opus Dei is not tied to any person, any group, any government, any political idea'. In an instruction drawn up for directors of Opus Dei, he directed them not to talk about politics and to show that in Opus Dei 'there is room for all opinions that respect the rights of the Church'. He added that the best guarantee that the directors will not interfere in matters of opinion is the members' awareness of their freedom, 'since if directors were to impose a specific criterion in temporal affairs, the other members who thought differently would immediately rebel, and rightly so. I would see myself having the sad duty of blessing and praising those who firmly refused to obey, and of correcting with holy indignation directors who wished to exercise an authority they can never have.'

One would need to know just how much Mgr. Escrivá had to give of himself to found Opus Dei to appreciate fully the heroism reflected in the following words of his: 'A long time ago I wrote that if Opus Dei had been involved in politics, even for an instant, in that moment of error I would have left Opus Dei. One can't give the slightest credit to a news item that has Opus Dei mixed up in political, economic or temporal affairs of any kind. On the one hand, the methods we use are always open, and our aims are always exclusively spiritual. On the other hand, the men and women of Opus Dei enjoy, in the choices open to them as citizens, complete personal freedom, respected by all, and consequently they are fully and personally responsible. It is therefore impossible for Opus Dei to be involved in activities that are not of a directly spiritual and apostolic nature, and so its activities are unconnected with the political life of any particular country. An Opus Dei mixed up in politics is a spectre that has never existed and will never exist. If this impossible situation were to occur, Opus Dei would fall apart immediately.'

The wide pluralism practised in Opus Dei causes no difficulties. As early as 1930 the founder wrote that this pluralism was 'a sign of good spirit, of the uprightness of our common action, and of respect for the legitimate freedom of each individual'. Members accept personal responsibility for their opinions and actions. Their spiritual link with the Prelature does not condition their political preferences in any way: thus there is a true pluralism.

It is worth noting that in Spain, in particular circumstances long since passed, the presence of three members in a Franco cabinet gave rise to interpretations that seemed to ignore the fact that, at the same time, other members of Opus Dei were in opposition and sometimes were victims of the arbitrariness of the same Franco government.

For most members of the Prelature, their involvement in politics is exactly the same as that of the majority of their fellow citizens: they assume their rights and their duties and express their opinions through the various channels open to them in their own political community. It is meaningless to say when referring to a person's political preferences (or his political activity if he is a politician) that he is a member of Opus Dei.

45

Asking whether one could talk of an Opus Dei 'conspiracy', a journalist from Le Monde, C. Vanhecke, observed in 1972: 'impartial observers think not. There would need to be some kind of ideology and there is none. This civic freedom its members enjoy seems to be the reason for its success'.

Respect for freedom of others

Members of Opus Dei who do choose to take an active part in political life do so in complete freedom. They receive no instructions or recommendations of any kind. Opus Dei's only influence is on the same level here as in work generally – to remind them of the need to act in accordance with their faith, which will be noticeable 'in the care you take to practise the supreme commandment of charity, overcoming all human passion, in the thoughtfulness with which you express your points of view as you study issues, avoiding heated arguments; by your respect for complete freedom of opinion in all spheres of human activity; by the understanding – frankness – with which you treat those persons who hold opposite views.'

This attitude of respect explains why you find in Opus Dei people of any and every political, intellectual and ideological tendency compatible with a Christian conscience. This variety also arises from the fact that the apostolate of Opus Dei is not restricted to persons of a particular social condition or way of thinking: it reaches out to all men of good will who wish to share in the apostolic work it proposes. Those who approach Opus Dei are drawn by the strength of a deeply loved faith, surmounting all human obstacles. In fact, the majority of members of the Prelature 'in all countries are labourers, housewives, shopkeepers, clerks, and so on, that is, people whose jobs carry no special political or social weight'.

Respect for freedom in temporal affairs must also extend to matters that do affect the faith and which for a Catholic are, logically, a matter of obedience to the Church. 'I don't understand the use of pressure to persuade or to impose' the founder said in this context. 'A person who has received the faith always feels that *he* is the victor. Error is fought by prayer, by God's grace, by talking things over calmly, by study, and by getting others to study! And by charity.'

Other spheres of freedom

(a) Research. Without labouring the point I would like to refer to what the founder has said about freedom in scientific research. In an address at a conferring of honorary degrees at the University of Navarre – on academics who included Professor Jean Roche, rector of the Sorbonne – in October 1967, Mgr. Escrivá recalled the university's role to serve man and be a leaven in society. 'It must seek truth in all spheres, in theology just as in the humanities and the natural sciences ... and in other branches of learning.'

The Christian attitude of a scientist consists in pursuing research with an open mind and no shirking of effort. This is not always easy. In a similar ceremony in 1974 in honour of Professor Jerome Lejeune of Paris and Mgr. Hengsbach, Bishop of Essen, Mgr. Escrivá declared that 'scientific objectivity rightly rejects all ideological neutrality, all ambiguity, all conformism, all cowardice: love of truth absorbs the entire life and work of a man of science'. He must beg for divine assistance, aware that the discovery of new knowledge is the fruit of the will of God who reveals himself to men.

To be truly scientific all research must necessarily lead to God. The founder did not mean by this that theology should invade the realm of academic research. On the contrary, he denounced any claims that would reduce the autonomy of scientific enquiry. This was a logical result of his love for personal freedom, for autonomy in temporal affairs, and for the rights of people to go about their work – in this case their search for truth – in an upright way.

Mgr. Escrivá defended 'the personal freedom of every layman to take, in the light of the principles established by the Church, all the (theoretical or practical) decisions he considers most appropri- i-

ate and most in line with his own personal convictions and apti-
tudes. These would include, for example, decisions regarding
different philosophical or political theories, different artistic or
cultural trends, or the problems of professional and social life.'

(b) Sacred Theology. In the more restricted sphere of theology,
members of Opus Dei can freely contribute to the apostolate of
doctrine by means of their research. They can enrich the treasury
of wisdom with new knowledge and suggest new solutions for
new problems. They accept in advance that they must submit to
the higher judgement of the Church and stay within the limits of
her teaching. They have exactly the same freedom as all other
Catholics to form their own opinions in philosophy, theology,
Holy Scripture, canon law, and so on. They can have disciples,
but they cannot form a school to which all the other members of
Opus Dei are obliged to belong. The creativity and freedom of
choice of each member is fully respected.

This being said, all the faithful of the Prelature respect the
general law of the Church which forbids the reading of books
harmful to faith and morals. Whenever, for good reasons – such
as research for a thesis – they need to read authors whose writings
can be harmful, they are quite happy to seek advice beforehand
and later to write review articles by which others can benefit
from their opinions.

Mgr. Escrivá often commented that the fully secular spirit and
approach of Opus Dei gave its members a special facility to inves-
tigate truth in freedom. That very freedom, united to charity,
leads them to desire and defend the personal freedom of all men.

What I have said about freedom would be incomplete if I did
not make one further point. When asked about the 'liberation'
the world craves for, the founder replied without the slightest
hesitation: 'Free yourself from sin. Free yourself from the chains
of your evil passions. Free yourself from vice. Free yourself from
bad company. Free yourself from indifference. Free yourself
from disfigurement of soul and body.' He himself fostered many
initiatives in favour of the underprivileged, but this did not
prevent him from saying that 'to want to free oneself from pain,

from poverty, from wretchedness is splendid, but it is not liberation. Liberation is the opposite. Liberation is ... to accept
suffering with joy, to accept illness gladly, to accept that stifling
cough with a smile!'

Personal responsibility

Underlying this affirmation of freedom, we always find in the
teachings of Mgr. Escrivá the other side of the coin – personal
responsibility. Freedom and responsibility are equally important,
he argued. They are like 'two parallel lines'. Without freedom
there can be no responsibility, and without responsibility there is
no freedom. Now that so many try to shrug off the consequences
of their deliberate acts, members of Opus Dei must be ready to
take full responsibility for their own actions, and all that follows
from them, since 'nobody can make our choices for us.'

For him it would be intolerable for a member of the Prelature,
or for any other Christian, to try to involve Opus Dei or the
Church, or to pretend to act in their name, when he is merely
expressing his own personal ideas. Legitimate though these might
be, they can never be put forward as dogma. No one has a right
to present as a doctrine of Opus Dei what is merely the outcome
of his personal reflection.

THE SPIRITUALITY OF OPUS DEI AND VATICAN II

The informed reader will have noticed that the aspects of Opus
Dei's spirituality described here are very reminiscent of certain
texts of the Second Vatican Council, notably chapters IV and V of
the dogmatic constitution *Lumen gentium*, which deal with the laity
and the universal call to holiness; the decree *Apostolicam actuosi-
tatem* on the apostolate of lay people; the dogmatic constitution
Gaudium et spes regarding the freedom and personal responsibility
of the Christian and the holiness of marriage; the decree

Presbyterorum ordinis on the priest and sanctity, etc. The Council said, for example, that 'it is quite clear that all Christians in any state or walk of life are called to the fullness of Christian life and to the perfection of love'. The laity have as their vocation 'to seek the kingdom of God by engaging in temporal affairs and directing them according to God's will'. Seeing in their daily work an 'extension of the Creator's work', they contribute to the consecration of the whole world to God and to the achievement of a 'higher sanctity, truly apostolic'. Indeed, 'the Christian vocation is, of its nature, a vocation to the apostolate . . . to be a leaven in the world'. Lay people 'strive to carry out their family, social and professional duties with such Christian generosity that their behaviour gradually permeates their environment and their work'.

These brief quotations from the Council – and they could be multiplied – echo the spirituality Mgr. Escrivá had been proposing since 1928. 'This is why he has been unanimously acknowledged as a precursor of the Council' (Cardinal Poletti, in the decree introducing the Cause of Beatification), as 'a pioneer of lay spirituality, opening up the path of holiness to men and women of all social conditions, anticipating, with the intuition of a holy instrument of God, the declarations that we read in the documents of the Second Vatican Council on the mission of the laity in the Church' (Cardinal Casariego, in a homily at the ordination of 54 members of Opus Dei). Similar expressions have been used by other churchmen. For example, Cardinal Pignedoli wrote of Mgr. Escrivá as 'a pioneer of lay spirituality and in many doctrinal aspects a precursor of the Second Vatican Council'. In his memoirs, Cardinal Frings refers to the criticism made of the founder of Opus Dei initially and to the joy he felt on seeing the Council 'take up his ideas and openly proclaim them'. Similarly Cardinal Baggio says that 'many thought it a heresy (to proclaim that sanctity was not the preserve of the privileged few) . . . but since Vatican II this thesis has become self evident. However, what continues to be revolutionary in the spiritual message of Mgr. Escrivá is the *practical manner* of guiding men and women, whatever their condition, the "man in the street", towards sanctity'. This is why, he adds, 'the life, work and message of Mgr. Escrivá constitute a turning point, or rather a new unpublished chapter, in Christian spirituality'. This chapter was opened on 2 October 1928, with the birth of Opus Dei, 'when he founded it in 1928 Mgr. Escrivá already anticipated much of what has become, with the Second Vatican Council, the common patrimony of the Church' (Cardinal Koenig).

Many other Council fathers have underlined this close link with the Council and it was to be extended in the subsequent establishment of Opus Dei as a personal Prelature. Finally in this connection let me quote something John Paul II said to members of Opus Dei during the Mass he celebrated for them in 1979: 'Your institution has as its objective the sanctification of ordinary life while remaining in the world, in one's own sphere of work and in one's profession: to live the Gospel in the world, living immersed in the world, but to transform it and redeem it through the love of Christ himself. Yours is truly a high ideal, for from the beginning it anticipated the theology of the laity which was to be a characteristic of the Church of the Council and after the Council.'

3: The Legal Structure of Opus Dei

THE SEARCH FOR THE RIGHT PLACE IN THE CHURCH

Something quite new

On 2 October 1928 Fr. Escrivá had seen quite clearly that 'sanctity is not something for the privileged few. Our Lord calls everyone, he expects Love from everyone; and that means everyone wherever they may be, whatever their calling, their job, or their position ... People do not have to leave their normal position in life to seek God ... since all paths of this earth can be an occasion for a meeting with Christ,' he wrote on 24 March 1930. Men and women of every race and culture and from every type of work and background are to seek sanctity and try to carry out an intense apostolate in and through their ordinary work. Opus Dei is a sort of general mobilisation of Christians who are attempting truly to take stock of the demands of Baptism, each carrying them out in the ordinary circumstances of secular life, reminding relatives, friends, colleagues, the people they meet and acquaintances, that 'they can be saints in the midst of all the noble concerns of this earth: sanctity is something that is accessible to all'. These men and women – intellectual and manual workers, married and single, etc, – were and continue to be, normal ordinary Christians who, with a stable dedication, by divine vocation and not according to a passing enthusiasm of the moment, try in this way to grow in their personal friendship with Christ. They strive to be contemplatives in the middle of the world and to make Christ known to others. He wrote on 19 March 1934 that his aim was not 'to solve the sad situation of the Church in Spain', nor was it to 'fulfil the particular need of any one country or period of time, because Jesus has wanted his Work from the very first moment to have a universal, catholic heart'.

From the very beginning he saw Opus Dei not as a temporary structure or organisation, but as something stable, with a characteristic unity of vocation, of formation, and of government. It was to be made up of a group or portion of the Lord's flock, eminently secular (having its own secular priests and ordinary layfolk), and it would be worldwide rather than defined by territorial boundaries.

His message was so new that it simply did not square with the form people expected of any new Church institution: they were used to either models based on the religious way of life (whenever there was any talk of 'vocation'), or associations of the faithful. The founder set about the task of working out the ascetical, juridical and theological doctrine and framework to fit his foundational charism. The 1917 Code of Canon Law was unable to accommodate such a charism; indeed in this it reflected the general teaching of the time which conceived the Church as structurally divided along lines defined by different states in life. But Fr. Escrivá was convinced Church law would ultimately devise a proper place for Opus Dei. Full of faith, in January 1932 he wrote to the first members: 'Remain faithful, and help me to be faithful and to be patient. We do not need to rush anything because, since our Lord has willed his Work, in his own time he will bring about the juridical solution, which cannot be seen at the moment; and Holy Church will recognise our divine way of serving her, which will be in the world . . . without any privileges, and maintaining the essence of our vocation. Nor will we be counted among the religious, since it is our Lord who does not wish this for us.' This last quote adds one more characteristic to the form the juridical solution would take: Opus Dei would find a place in the *general* Law of the Church, a place which would accommodate other institutions as well, and so it would not occupy a position based on exception or privilege. As Fr. Escrivá saw it, law followed life: in the history of the Church, he pointed out, it was not a matter of rigid, prefabricated rules to which life had to conform; the Church was a living, divine body endowed with charisms by the Holy Spirit; law was at the service of charism, not the other way round. Therefore, his policy was to press on with his work, supporting this with prayer and mortification, putting his trust in God. Everything would fit into place in due course.

In the first years of the foundation he saw that this general mobilisation of Christians, which had its own method of training and rules, needed a structure or organisation designed for ordinary Christians: something secular, personal, and based on a charism or special vocation from God, which would specify and develop the vocation which is common to all Christians and which has its origin in Baptism. A small episode illustrates quite clearly the direction in which his mind was working in his search for this juridical solution. One day in 1936 Pedro Casciaro, a member of the Work, now a priest, was waiting for the founder in the church of Santa Isabel in Madrid, and began translating to himself the inscriptions on two tombstones at his feet. Just then Fr. Josemaría came out of the sacristy and pointing to the slabs said: 'That is where the eventual juridical solution of the Work can be found.' The slabs carried the epitaphs of two prelates who had held a unique and wide-ranging ecclesiastical jurisdiction of a secular type, and which was not territorial but personal. The founder would still have to sow his seed far and wide before such a formula could become a reality; this formula would not be a kind of privilege (literally a 'private law') designed for the jurisdiction enjoyed by the two priests mentioned; it would be a personal, non-territorial, structure, in the general law of the Church, open to people of all professions, languages, cultures and social classes.

THE APPROVALS OF THE HIERARCHY OF THE CHURCH

Diocesan approvals

Being a man who profoundly respected the authority of the Church, Fr. Escrivá always wished to show in words and in deeds his submission to the hierarchy, since it alone, with the assistance of the Holy Spirit, is competent to judge the authenticity of different charisms: 'Do not stifle the utterances of the Spirit . . . and yet you must scrutinise it all carefully, retaining only what is good' (1 Thess 5:19–21). This is why when he began his work he counted always on the permission and encouragement of his bishop, the Bishop of Madrid, Mgr. Leopoldo Eijo y Garay and also of his Vicar General, Don Francisco Moran. The complete novelty of this new pastoral phenomenon gave rise to a whole series of misunderstandings which grew with the development of the apostolate of Opus Dei. When these misunderstandings became more organised and systematic the Bishop of Madrid felt the Work needed some kind of formal ecclesiastical approval and suggested Fr. Escrivá have it established as a Pious Union, which was a form of association of the faithful established in the Code of that time. Mgr. Eijo y Garay granted this approval on 19 March 1941.

Even in 1928 the founder had foreseen that there would be priests in Opus Dei, and he realised that it needed priests of its own as soon as possible, who would come from among the lay members, and have not only a good ecclesiastical training but also plenty of professional experience in secular work, and would be well formed in the spirit of Opus Dei. Such priests would be able to provide the specific spiritual attention and the doctrinal and religious formation needed by the growing number of members of the Work. Church law decreed that nobody could be ordained unless their life-long financial upkeep with minimum dignity could be guaranteed; and also there was the question of juridical stability. This legal assurance is known as the 'title of ordination'.

None of the titles envisaged for secular priests were applicable to the Work. Our Lord provided a solution on 14 February 1943: within Opus Dei priests would be able to have their title of ordination under the Priestly Society of the Holy Cross, of which they would be members.

At the request of the Bishop of Madrid, the Holy See in 1943 gave a mild form of approval (the 'appositio manuum' is the technical description). A *nihil obstat* was granted on 11 October 1943 to enable the Bishop of Madrid to give official status to the small group of members of Opus Dei who were training for the priesthood, and set them up as a society of common life without vows. On 8 December 1943 canonical status was granted to the Priestly Society of the Holy Cross. The founder of the Work was very careful to point out in various documents that the term 'common life' was not to be understood in the canonical sense but rather in a new and wider sense. In other words it was to be understood as a unity or a community of spirit and not in the physical sense of living under the same roof. With this and other clarifications he was able to safeguard the secular character of the priests, and he was very careful to ensure that the juridical form, rather than smothering the charism, would enable Opus Dei 'to move forward, safeguarding the essential, which cannot be changed', as he wrote on 14 February 1944. This development was simply a step in the right direction. The other members of Opus Dei, both men and women, continued to be ordinary Christians, secular lay people who formed their own association of the faithful, inseparably united to the Priestly Society of the Holy Cross.

On 14 February 1944 the founder once again reaffirmed in writing that Opus Dei is not 'a new version of the religious state, adapted to present circumstances'; he was not trying to create 'a new canonical status', which would be 'something completely contrary to the essence of our vocation ... It is precisely the opposite; in other words, you have to retain the same state in life you had when the divine call to Opus Dei came to you.'

The same letter of 1944 explained why the Priestly Society of the Holy Cross had been established. After referring to the reasons already given – the need for priests, and specifically priests who would come from within the ranks of Opus Dei – he added a further reason. This is something he had explained in earlier documents, for example in his Letter of 1 April 1934. He said that these priests would 'have some responsibilities of government ... a fundamental point in the very constitution of the Work ... strictly necessary for the juridical form which is appropriate for us'. These words give us a glimpse of the fact that the founder was thinking of an ecclesiastical structure in which priests and lay people would form a unity, but in which the principal positions of authority, which would be positions within an ecclesiastical structure, would need to be held by priests and would require the ministerial priesthood.

The solution of having a society of common life without vows, together with an association of the faithful inseparably linked to it, was 'the only viable solution within the limits available in the established law, and so we are ready to give way in the matter of words, provided that ... we affirm in a precise way the true nature of our way'. It is a solution that is 'necessarily transitory, although it may have to do for some time, and it will be superseded as soon as a different juridical route becomes available'. The founder did not hide the difficulties implied by this new juridical arrangement and remarked: 'This solution is uncomfortable because the main thing – Opus Dei – appears in second place.'

Now he was able to count on a group of the faithful, ordinary Christians, with priests to look after them, and who later could occupy positions of authority. Up to this point, the framework in which Opus Dei was set was a diocesan one. To spread out, it needed a wider approval, from the Holy See.

Approvals of the Holy See

In 1946 the founder sent to Rome Fr. Alvaro del Portillo, one of his first priests, to negotiate for pontifical approval. He was to try to obtain a juridical statute of universal right which, among other things, would make it clear that the priests incardinated in the Priestly Society of the Holy Cross and the lay members of Opus Dei formed a single organic and indivisible pastoral entity. On acquainting himself with the newness of Opus Dei a high-ranking prelate of the Roman Curia commented: 'You have come a century too soon.' In spite of being seriously ill, the founder travelled to Rome in June of that same year to pursue the matter.

Since 1940 studies had been going on in the Roman Curia to develop a new legal structure to accommodate various new apostolic initiatives, particularly certain associations of 'consecrated lay people' founded by Fr. Gemelli, OFM, of Milan. Since no other suitable solution existed, the founder of Opus Dei agreed to a suggestion to come under a proposed Apostolic Constitution which was already in advanced draft form, to enable the Work to get the necessary statute of pontifical right. He was assured that the new kind of grouping would be a 'more secular' form than the Societies of common life without vows, which were equivalent to the religious Institutes. In the meantime the Holy See granted a series of spiritual benefits to the members of Opus Dei with the apostolic brief *Cum Societatis* of 28 June 1946. On 13 August of the same year a document came out which was an 'approval of the aims' of Opus Dei and which highlighted the 'sanctity' of the Work. On 2 February 1947 Pope Pius XII established Secular Institutes through the Apostolic Constitution *Provida Mater Ecclesia*.

(a) The 'Decretum Laudis' of 1947. Part of this Constitution was open to a theological interpretation at variance with the foundational charism of Opus Dei. For example, even though the secularity of these Institutes was clearly expressed, the constitution described them as religious 'quoad substantiam' and it required, as a condition for the approval of an Institute, the so-called 'consecrated life', involving profession of the three evangelical counsels of poverty, chastity and obedience taken as sacred bonds, or vows, or pledges. Years earlier the founder had written: 'We are interested in all the virtues ... but we are not interested in promises or vows, even though these are theologically worthy of every respect, and indeed we regard them in others with great respect' (8 December 1941).

Nevertheless the spread of Opus Dei required it to cease to be an institution of purely diocesan right and become one of pontifical right; this would give it a universal and centralised juridical framework capable of guaranteeing unity in its government and spirit, in accordance with its apostolic growth and development.

Since it was impossible to find a better formula among existing laws, the Holy See, at the request of the founder, established Opus Dei as a Secular Institute, in the Decree *Primum Institutum* of 24 February 1947. This approval gave the Work the universal juridical framework noted above, and also it confirmed its faculty to incardinate priests.

On 29 December 1947 the founder wrote, describing this new development: 'Once again, in our effort to see our juridical position crystallise, to get closer to the model we need, I have been forced to accept certain things, in the letter and within what is possible; but always waiting for everything to work out better next time, until we reach the ideal juridical position which will enable us to serve the Church and souls without any fear of our spirit being frustrated by unsuitable laws.' In the same letter he added: 'Up to now we have gone where we never wished to go, though convinced that these wanderings are the route God wants us to take . . . in the firm conviction and hope that everything will work out, because it is for the good of the Church and of society. We must, however, pray to our Lord to provide the right solution, and we must take all the steps necessary to get off this sidetrack and start walking along the wide and sure road. When that moment comes some people may tell us that the track – this one which we are walking along right now – cannot be moved. It most certainly can! Every path can be moved, every human position can be changed, even if they have been in use for centuries.' Throughout the letter he frequently adverts to the danger that the provisions of *Provida Mater Ecclesia* might in practice gradually become more equivalent to a 'religious state', and that 'then our position would become much more uncomfortable and perhaps intolerable.'

Besides, the structure of the Secular Institute could accommodate other aspects of Opus Dei only by making them an exception to the general rule and by granting certain privileges. This was distasteful to the founder. Two such aspects in particular were: firstly, unity, not only of spirit and formation, but also of jurisdiction and government, for men and women, priests and lay people of the Work, ordinary Christians; secondly, identity and fullness of vocation of *all* members, irrespective of family situation and other personal circumstances, and irrespective of availability to help in organised apostolic projects over and above the personal apostolate of each one in his own environment.

(b) The Decree Primum Inter of 1950. However, the juridical progress of the Work had to go ahead, extending the legal framework so as to contain everything which the Lord was asking for, and also trying to silence, or at least attenuate, the organised campaign of misrepresentation of Opus Dei which had now reached Rome. On 8 December 1949 Mgr. Escrivá wrote: 'In conscience we cannot but move ahead, making sure we overcome this compromise, that is to say, we have to give way without giving in; we must leave things in God's hands; he writes straight with crooked lines; he will enable us to reach our goal'. For this reason, on 11 February 1950, he asked the Holy See for another approval. On 16 June 1950, with the recommendation of 110 prelates from 17 countries, including twelve Cardinals, the Decree *Primum Inter* gave its approval to the legal norms governing Opus Dei, and at the same time – as the founder sought – to the basic characteristics of the spirit of the Work. This spirit was the key to the correct interpretation of the legal norms, which were still not appropriate for the charismatic reality of the Work.

This approval gave Opus Dei greater stability, scope for apostolic activity, and means to defend itself. Its fully secular spirit was approved in a much clearer way, as also the position of the Priestly Society of the Holy Cross, so that the unity between priests and lay members was underlined. Also, although not yet in a fully satisfactory way, juridical entry into Opus Dei was given to people who for long had belonged to Opus Dei in spirit but not in fact – people of every walk of life, married, widowed and celibate. Non-Catholics and even non-Christians were admitted as co-operators. Priests incardinated in different dioceses were able to join the Priestly Society of the Holy Cross, to receive spiritual help from it, without any detriment to canonical and ministerial links with their respective bishops.

A very important advance had been made. Some problems remained however, and there was always the risk of other difficulties arising due to the kind of general interpretation being given to the norms governing Secular Institutes, interpretations often taking, as point of departure, the religious state or, in a wider sense, the 'state of perfection' or the 'state of consecrated life'. To protect Opus Dei from this danger, a rescript was issued by the Sacred Congregation for Religious on 2 August 1950 granting the founder of Opus Dei and his Council permission to propose to the Holy See modifications and additions to the approved legal Norms, when this appeared necessary and suitable for the development, needs and extension of its 'excellent and unique apostolate'.

(c) *Inappropriateness of the Secular Institute formula*. Clearly, approval as a Secular Institute was unsatisfactory, all the more so because of the widespread and growing tendency to view members of Secular Institutes as members of a modern kind of religious order, and to apply to them criteria proper to religious. Nevertheless, out of a sense of loyalty to the Church, Mgr. Escrivá wrote on 24 December 1951 that 'for as long as there is no danger of deforming our spirit ... we have to defend the juridical form of the Secular Institute for as long as it is feasible in conscience to do so.'

This letter of 24 December 1951 is a particularly significant document. Referring to the future definitive juridical solution, he wrote: 'I do not know, I repeat, when the time will come for the proper juridical solution, for which I pray so much and for which I urge you to pray ... I do not know when this moment will be and I imagine it will take many years, yet I am absolutely sure that it will come ... I will not accept a solution which involves exceptions or privileges, but rather a canonical formula which will enable us to work in such a way that the reverend bishops, whom we love "in deed and in truth", will continue to be grateful for our work. The rights of the bishops will remain as now, quite firm and secure, and at last we will be able to follow our path of love, of commitment and of dedication without useless obstacles being placed in the way of our service to the Church, that is to say, service to the Pope, to the dioceses, and to all souls ... When this final and truly decisive juridical solution is promulgated, our situation has to be absolutely clear: we are not religious nor can we be considered in any way equivalent to them. We are Christians who live consistently with our faith, and who are ready to put it into practice at every opportunity. The lay people will do this by means of a normal civil contract [with Opus Dei] and they will practise Christian virtues in line with the spirit and statutes of the Work. They will undertake to do this for a certain period of time or for life. The priests additionally will have to live the consequences which derive from their priestly ordination and their incardination into the Work'. This text foreshadows, as do many others from Mgr. Escrivá, a canonical formula which did not exist at that time, but which would come into being with the personal Prelature.

In several later documents addressed to his sons and daughters the founder of Opus Dei repeats these same ideas. One could mention in particular a letter of 19 March 1954 in which he says: 'We are not in fact a Secular Institute; neither do we form an "association of the faithful" whose members have no mutual or permanent bond with their respective society; nor can we be confused with the so-called "apostolic movements".' Then again on 2 October 1958, writing on the thirtieth anniversary of the founding of Opus Dei, after pointing out the reasons why 'in fact we are not a Secular Institute and will not in the future describe ourselves as such', he spoke of his decision to ask for a new juridical status from the Holy See. 'I shall inform the Holy See at the appropriate moment about this situation, about this concern. At the same time I will make known that we ardently desire that a suitable solution be found, which will not involve granting us a privilege — something repugnant to our spirit and outlook — nor will it change our present relationship with the bishop of each place.'

At the same time as he wrote these reflections to his sons and daughters, he informed the Holy See, both verbally and in writing, of the difficulties the present situation was creating. For example, only weeks after asking for the 1950 approval he had to express his respectful and firm protest against a recent decree in which the Sacred Congregation of the Council renewed its prohibition on priests and religious engaging in business, and specified that this law also applied 'to members of the recent Secular Institutes'. At times he sought provisional solutions through the granting of favours and dispensations; however, although these averted one difficulty or another, they meant that Opus Dei was being treated 'differently', gradually acquiring an extraordinary or unique legal status, contrary to the express desire of the founder.

PREPARING THE DEFINITIVE JURIDICAL SOLUTION

The early 60s

As we have seen, by the early 1960s Opus Dei had an organisational structure of universal ambit, with a centralised government presided over by the founder, whom the Holy See had granted an authority which, for all practical purposes, was jurisdictional. The institution likewise had its own specific apostolic task, clearly secular and lay, namely, to help people understand and respond to the universal call to sanctity, and in particular sanctity in and through ordinary work, carried out with a contemplative and apostolic spirit. To carry out this mission, Opus Dei counted on a portion or grouping of the faithful – clergy and lay, men and women, married and single etc. – who formed together an organic pastoral unity, all sharing the one vocation. However, this unique charismatic and social reality, which was without precedence in the history of the Church, was not adequately institutionalised.

The founder set about seeking a definitive solution, trusting in God and in the intercession of our Lady and also counting on the prayers and mortifications that all his sons and daughters had been offering continually for his intention for many years. He was also urged on by his own conscience – he felt he had a duty as founder to see God's will carried out – and by the signs of the times, which seemed ripe: the Second Vatican Council was about to begin . . .

On 5 March 1960, Pope John XXIII received Mgr. Escrivá and Fr. Alvaro del Portillo in audience. On 14 March they were received by Cardinal Domenico Tardini, the Secretary of State, and on 9 April Fr. Alvaro del Portillo presented the Cardinal Secretary of State with a petition to set in motion the juridical solution capable of resolving the institutional problem affecting Opus Dei. Already in this petition mention was made of a prelature and of its coming under the Sacred Consistorial Congregation, now the Congregation for Bishops. There was no official reply. The founder was very happy despite this silence because, as he said, 'a seed has been sown and it cannot fail to bear fruit'. On 7 January 1962 a new formal petition was presented to Pope John XXIII on the advice of Cardinal Pietro Ciriaci. The founder took all these steps despite strong interior resistance because, as a good lawyer, he realised that the existing law would need to be stretched considerably to accommodate prelatures of a personal nature. Pope John XXIII instructed that the petition be replied to by saying it could not be dealt with because it did not fit in with existing legislation. The reply was interlocutory in character, for already the preparations for the Second Vatican Council were opening the way for a new legal structure, now known as a personal prelature.

Pope John XXIII died in June 1963. When Pope Paul VI was elected, the founder of the Work, both directly and through Fr. Alvaro del Portillo, renewed his negotiations with the Holy See. On 24 January 1964 the new Pope received Mgr. Escrivá for the first time in a private and very cordial audience: they had known one another since 1946. Within a few days (on 14 February) the founder sent the Holy Father a letter in which, among many other topics, he pointed out the need for a solution for the institutional problems of Opus Dei, although without presenting an official request. The Pope had an answer sent to him which implied that the basis of a solution to the problem lay in the Council documents. In each of these approaches to the Holy See a very clear statement of the founder emerges that no type of privileged arrangement was being sought, and that he wanted relations with the diocesan Bishops to remain substantially the same as before, without any detriment to their rights. In a letter of 25 May 1962 he wrote a letter detailing these and other characteristics of the possible solution.

The Second Vatican Council

The Second Vatican Council, and the legal documents applying the conciliar decrees, effectively opened up a suitable juridical path in the general legislation of the Church.

The Decree *Presbyterorum ordinis*, of 7 December 1965, says that it may be useful to create personal Prelatures 'for particular pastoral activities for various social groups at regional, national or worldwide level'. This section 10 of the decree was made operational by Pope Paul VI, by his Motu Proprio *Ecclesiae Sanctae*, of 6 August 1966. This document states that, in order to carry out particular pastoral or missionary tasks, the Holy See may find it useful to establish prelatures of this kind, made up of priests of the secular clergy, governed by their own prelate and having their own statutes. As well as laying down rules regarding the duties of the prelate towards his own clergy and the relations between the prelature and the ecclesiastical authorities, Paul VI adds that 'there is no reason why lay people, single or married, who have made an agreement with the prelature, should not dedicate themselves to the service of the works and initiatives of the prelature, using their professional talents'.

On 15 August 1967, the Apostolic Constitution *Regimini Ecclesiae Universae*, which reorganised the Roman Curia, foresaw that personal Prelatures would be subject to the Sacred Congregation for Bishops.

An intermediate phase

In 1969, Mgr. Escrivá called a special General Congress of Opus Dei, after informing Pope Paul VI of his intention and with his encouragement. Studies were then initiated to effect the change of Opus Dei into a personal Prelature, in accordance with the nature of Opus Dei and the ordinances of the Vatican Council. The founder drafted new statutes, in readiness for the time when it would be suitable to present them to the Holy See.

These studies were not interrupted either by the death of Mgr. Escrivá in 1975, or by that of Paul VI three years later. They received confirmation and encouragement from John Paul I and John Paul II. On 3 March 1979, Pope John Paul II asked the Sacred Congregation for Bishops, whose responsibility it was to study the matter, to examine Opus Dei's request, and to take into account 'all the data of law and of fact'.

In an article published in *L'Osservatore Romano*, 28 November 1982, the Congregation's Prefect, Cardinal Baggio, explained what this involved: 'Data of law', because, since the Motu Proprio contains norms for a general law or fundamental statute for personal Prelatures, what was being requested was not the concession of a privilege (which besides Opus Dei had not asked for), but an attentive evaluation of those general norms to see whether it would be correct to apply them in the specific case we were studying, and 'Data of fact', because the setting up of the Prelature was to be the result, not of abstract doctrinal specula-tion, but rather and above all, of a careful consideration of an already existing apostolic and pastoral entity, that is, Opus Dei, the legitimacy and soundness of whose foundational charism had often been recognised by ecclesiastical authority.

This study took three and a half years and went through four stages:

(a) a working session of the General Assembly of the Congregation, on 28 June 1979, examined the matter in general:

(b) a technical committee was set up, which met twenty-five times between 27 February 1980 and 19 February 1981, and

studied all aspects of the matter – historical, juridical, pastoral, doctrinal, apostolic, institutional and procedural;

(c) the Holy Father studied the conclusions of this committee which took up two volumes totalling some 600 pages and included the proposed statutes of the future prelature. John Paul II decided to submit these conclusions to the collegial deliberation of a special committee of Cardinals. This committee gave its reply on 26 September 1981;

(d) before proceeding to the establishment of the prelature, the Pope decided that a note outlining the essential characteristics of the prelature should be sent to the bishops in countries where Opus Dei was working through canonically erected centres, that is, to more than 2000 bishops, with the purpose of informing them and allowing them – with plenty of time to do so – to make any observations or suggestions they saw fit. These communications were few in number and were studied carefully and given detailed replies. At the same time, the statutes drafted by Mgr. Escrivá were further examined. 'This study confirmed their validity and soundness, and showed clearly the foundational charism of the Servant of God and his great love for the Church' (Mgr. Costalunga).

This lengthy study having removed 'all doubts about the grounds for, the possibility of, and the specific form of an affirmative reply to the request, the suitability and usefulness of the desired transformation of Opus Dei into a personal Prelature became quite apparent' (John Paul II).

The erection of Opus Dei as a personal Prelature

On 5 August 1982, Pope John Paul II approved a Declaration of the Sacred Congregation for Bishops which explained the fundamental traits of the Prelature as contained in its particular laws approved by the Holy See. On 23 August, the Pope's decision to erect Opus Dei as a personal prelature was made public. On 28 November of the same year, L'Osservatore Romano published the Declaration signed by the Prefect of the Sacred Congregation for

Bishops and by its Secretary, Mgr. Moreira Neves; an article by Cardinal Baggio entitled 'A benefit for the whole Church'; and a commentary, 'The erection of Opus Dei as a personal Prelature', signed by the Under-Secretary of the Congregation, Mgr. Costalunga.

On 25 January 1983, the Pope promulgated the new Code of Canon Law which contains a special section (canons 294–297) on personal Prelatures.

The official inauguration of the Prelature of the Holy Cross and Opus Dei took place on 19 March 1983 in the Basilica of St Eugenio in Rome. The Pope's Nuncio in Italy, Archbishop Romolo Carboni, represented the Pope. The ceremony consisted of the promulgation and handing over of the Apostolic Constitution *Ut sit*, of 28 November 1982, by which Opus Dei was erected as a personal Prelature. The Constitution also promulgates the Statutes (or particular code of law) of Opus Dei.

On 2 May 1983 the *Acta Apostolicae Sedis* published the Apostolic Constitution *Ut sit* and the Declaration (vol. 75, pages 423–425; 464–468).

THE CANONICAL STATUS OF PERSONAL PRELATURES

Personal prelatures in general

Personal prelatures are juridical structures which have a clearly personal character (that is to say, they are not normally constituted on the basis of a defined territory) and they are secular. They are set up by the Holy See to carry out specific pastoral activities within a region, a country, or throughout the world.

To fulfil its specific pastoral tasks, each prelature always has its own Prelate, who is its ordinary, whether he is actually a bishop or not, and in addition secular priests, who receive their training in the seminaries of the prelature. It is foreseen that lay people, through agreements made with the prelature, may devote themselves to its different activities and initiatives in a manner established by the particular laws in each case.

The Council documents and the more explicit subsequent pontifical documents indicate, among other things, that the setting up of personal prelatures should come about after consulting the episcopal conferences of the territories concerned. This is done in line with the procedures laid down for each of these institutions and following their own particular statutes given by the Holy See. These statutes are required, moreover, to fulfil a further stipulation of the Council: namely, that the laws governing each prelature always respect the rights of the diocesan bishops, to ensure that the activity of each prelature is harmoniously integrated into the pastoral work of the universal Church and of the local churches (cf. *Pontifical Yearbook*).

Within the juridical structure of the Church, personal prelatures perform a pastoral function which can be carried out in a particular diocese only with the prior agreement of the respective bishop.

These characteristics distinguish personal prelatures both from particular churches (or dioceses) and from associative institutions (institutes of consecrated life, societies of apostolic life, associations of the faithful). This is so even though a personal prelature has some of the same constitutive elements as a diocese (prelate, incardinated secular clergy, and in this case, lay people who take full part in the apostolic activities of the prelature and who form its *coetus christifidelium*); and even though there is no reason why an associative phenomenon would not later give rise to a personal prelature.

Personal prelatures belong to the common law of the Church. This is seen for example from the way they appear in the Code of Canon Law. As such, they are not based on privilege or exemption unlike the territorial prelatures in the 1917 Code, and personal dioceses based on the principle of complete independence or autonomy from the local churches and the respective diocesan bishops.

The Opus Dei Prelature

(A) *Its Nature*. It is a personal Prelature with its own Statutes, of international scope, with its central offices in Rome, and depends on the Sacred Congregation for Bishops. The Oratory of Our Lady of Peace, where its founder is buried, in the central offices of Opus Dei, at 75 Viale Bruno Buozzi, Rome, has been erected as the prelatic church.

The proper ordinary of the Prelature is its Prelate. He has ordinary power of jurisdiction over the clergy incardinated in the Prelature and over the laity incorporated into it; for the latter this jurisdiction extends only to the carrying out of the specific obligations they have undertaken as a result of a juridical bond stemming from a contract with the Prelature. Both clergy and laity depend on the Prelate's authority in carrying out the specific apostolic tasks of the Prelature.

(a) The clergy or *presbyterium* of the Prelature is made up exclusively of priests who have come from among the lay members of Opus Dei. Thus no priest or candidate for the priesthood is taken from any diocese. The priests of Opus Dei depend exclusively on their Prelate, but they must observe the norms issued by the diocesan Bishops for the general discipline of the clergy and also all the territorial dispositions which are applicable to the generality of the Catholic faithful.

(b) The laity of the Prelature can be men or women, single or married, from all levels of society, from every occupation and family situation. They receive a specific vocation to dedicate themselves to the particular apostolic tasks of Opus Dei. They depend on the local Bishop, as defined by ecclesiastical law, just like other members of the faithful — no different from them — in accordance with the statutes of the Prelature. They depend on the Prelate solely for things that refer to the purposes of Opus Dei.

(c) The relations between the Prelature and the territorial ecclesiastical hierarchy are laid down in the Statutes, as the Code of Canon Law prescribes for such cases (can. 297). The diocesan

bishop must be informed before the Prelature begins regular activities in his territory. His agreement is a condition *sine qua non* for the erection of a centre of the Prelature. He has the right to visit centres erected canonically, to inspect the oratory, tabernacle and place for confessions. The priests of the Prelature need faculties from him to carry out their ministry to faithful who do not belong to the Prelature. In each country the Prelature must maintain frequent and regular contact with the president of the Episcopal Conference and with the bishops in whose dioceses it works. And, should a Bishop wish to entrust a parish to the Prelature, he will enter into an agreement with the Prelature.

(B) *Its Purpose*. A document of the Holy See makes clear that the Prelature of Opus Dei has a double purpose:

'The Prelate and his clergy carry out a particular pastoral work in the service of the Prelature's laity, who are clearly defined; while the whole Prelature, clergy and laity together, engage in a specific apostolate in the service of the universal Church and of the local Churches.

'There are, therefore, two fundamental aspects of the structure and purpose of the Prelature, which constitute its *raison d'être*, and explain how it fits naturally into the whole of the pastoral and evangelising activity of the Church:

(a) On the one hand, the particular pastoral work which the Prelate with his clergy undertakes, in assisting and sustaining the lay faithful incorporated into Opus Dei in the fulfilment of the specific ascetical, formative and apostolic commitments they have taken on, which are particularly demanding;

(b) on the other hand, the apostolate which the clergy and laity of the Prelature, inseparably united, carry out in helping to bring about, in all sectors of society, a deep consciousness of the universal call to holiness and apostolate and, more specifically, an awareness of the sanctifying value of ordinary work.'

Priests already incardinated in dioceses do not form part of the clergy of the Prelature. They may join the Priestly Society of the Holy Cross, an association of clergy which is inseparably united to the Prelature, erected by the Holy See at the same time as the Prelature. These priests receive a new vocation to seek holiness by carving out their pastoral ministry according to the spirit of Opus Dei. Their diocesan status remains unchanged, as does their dependence on their respective Bishop. They have no internal superior in the Priestly Society of the Holy Cross, so no problems of double obedience can arise. As is true of every association, they are subject to the internal regulations of the association which, in this case, refer only to their spiritual lives. The Prelate of Opus Dei is the President General of the Association.

INTERNAL ORGANISATION

Central government

The Prelate is elected for life by an elective Congress called for this purpose. The election requires papal confirmation. The Prelate must be a priest with at least five years of ministerial experience. He may appoint an auxiliary vicar.

The Prelature of Opus Dei is an organic and indivisible pastoral entity. It carries out its apostolates through its men's section, and its women's section. The Prelate, who is the Ordinary of the Prelature, governs both sections with the help of his councils. This unity of government ensures the fundamental unity of spirit and jurisdiction between the two sections.

The Prelate is aided in his work of governing the men's section by a General Council made up of an auxiliary vicar, if appointed, the vicar general, the vicar for the women's section (called the central priest secretary), three deputy secretaries, one delegate (at least) from each of the regions, the prefect of studies and the general administrator. The auxiliary vicar, vicar general and central priest secretary are all chosen from the priest members. A procurator, who must be a priest, represents the Prelature at the Holy See, and a central spiritual director watches over the common spiritual direction of all the faithful of the Prelature, under the direction of the Prelate and his councils.

The women's section is governed by the Prelate with his auxiliary vicar, the vicar general, the central priest secretary and the Central Advisory, a similar entity to the General Council of the men's section and with similar functions.

All the directors of these two organs of government are appointed for an eight-year term (with the exception of the auxiliary vicar).

Regional and local government

The Prelate, with the agreement of his councils, sets up regions or quasi-regions, which are governed by a regional vicar, who is appointed by the Prelate with the agreement of his council, and who is assisted by a council for each section. These two councils are organised in a similar way to the central councils.

Every canonically erected centre of the Prelature is governed by a director with his committee.

There can also be intermediate organs of government between the regional vicar with his councils, and the centres: these are called delegations, and help the government of the Prelature within a portion of the territory that makes up a region. Delegations are governed by a vicar delegate, who is a priest, aided by a council.

4: Members of Opus Dei

WHERE THE MEMBERS COME FROM

Oneness of vocation, plurality of members

To join Opus Dei requires a true, supernatural vocation. It is a personal intimate calling from God to put the whole of one's life at his service, in accordance with the spirituality of Opus Dei, and taking into account each person's particular circumstances in the world.

(A) *One single vocation.* On numerous occasions Mgr. Escrivá stressed how all members of Opus Dei receive the very same calling to holiness and apostolate in the exercise of their work; and that, consequently, there are not different levels of members, in the sense of some members being more important than others or receiving a more demanding vocation. He emphasised complete equality. In Opus Dei there are priests and laity, men and women, young and less young, single, married and widowed. The lay members come from all levels of society, and from all races, and work in the most varied professions. Opus Dei, when it has reached its maturity in a country, has a social and occupational cross-section very typical of the country in question.

The identity of vocation means that, in practice, all the faithful of the Prelature take on the same ascetic and apostolic commitments and receive the same doctrinal preparation. This oneness of vocation also extends to the priests of the Prelature. It is important to notice the way in which the common priesthood of all the faithful and the ministerial priesthood of the clergy complement one another, to achieve the one apostolic purpose of Opus Dei.

(B) *Diversity of members.* Within this single vocation – imaginatively described by the founder as a single 'cooking pot' into which everyone can dip according to his needs – there is a variety of types of members: basically a reflection of the personal circumstances and the other responsibilities of those who ask to be members of the Prelature.

(a) The *numeraries* are priests and laypeople who have received a call from God to live apostolic celibacy. They put all their efforts and their complete availability into carrying out the specific apostolic tasks of Opus Dei. Normally they live in centres of the Prelature, so that they can look after the formation of the other faithful of the Prelature and direct apostolic activities.

(b) The *associates* are lay faithful of the Prelature who place their entire lives at the service of God in apostolic celibacy, according to the spirit of Opus Dei. But their long-term personal, family or professional circumstances lead them normally to live with their own families.

(c) The *supernumeraries* are lay faithful, either single or married, who give themselves fully to God in their particular state in life – having the same divine vocation as the numeraries and associates. They play a full part in the apostolates of Opus Dei, insofar as this is compatible with their family, professional and social obligations. Like all the other faithful of the Prelature they transform their occupations and their social relationships into means of sanctification and apostolate. But, like the associates, they do this in their homes and in keeping with their family duties.

(d) There are also *co-operators*, who are not actually members of Opus Dei. They help its apostolic activities with their prayers, donations, gifts, and even their work. They participate in the spiritual benefits of Opus Dei, and make up an Association which is ultimately linked with the Prelature. Non-Catholics and even non-Christians can be co-operators.

Priests

(A) *The clergy of the Prelature.* The clergy of the Prelature are drawn from lay members who, after third level civil studies, have followed the prescribed ecclesiastical studies (to doctorate level in one of the sacred sciences) and have then been called to the priesthood by the Prelate. They come from the ranks of the Prelature and are trained within it. Opus Dei does not, therefore, take any priests, or candidates for the priesthood, away from dioceses.

These members then give up the profession they have practised perhaps for many years, to become 'priest-priests, neither more nor less priests, but priests one hundred per cent', following the express wish of the founder. The vocation of Opus Dei is the same for all; and so, for a member of Opus Dei, the priesthood is not a kind of crowning of his career. It is a call to continue serving souls, though in a different way from the laity.

The priests of Opus Dei receive their training in centres which the Prelature erects for this purpose, following the norms laid down by the Holy See. The Prelate, either personally or through his vicars, gives the priests their canonical mission and their priestly faculties first and foremost to look after the activities and the faithful of the Prelature. This includes the Sacrament of Penance or Reconciliation, respecting, of course, the right of each person to go to any confessor he wishes. In addition to this pastoral care of lay members, the clergy of the Prelature, like all the faithful, also carry out extensive and deep apostolic work in the service of the Universal Church and of the local Churches; they foster a recognition of the universal call to holiness in the carrying out of one's everyday work.

The Prelate must provide for the adequate support of his clergy and for their care in case of sickness, incapacity, or old age. He also encourages them to keep close links with the clergy of the territory in which they exercise their ministry, and to live a deep fraternity with them. The priests of the Prelature feel themselves to be – as they are in fact – diocesan priests in whichever diocese they work. They belong by full right to the diocesan *presbyterium*.

The clergy of the Prelature numbered around 1700 in the year 2000. Ordinations take place regularly and involve, in recent years, some sixty priests annually. Ordination to the priesthood has been conferred notably by Cardinals Jubany (1974), Casariego (1975), Koenig (1978), Hoffner (1979), Oddi (1980) and Etchegaray (1981) and by the present Pope (June and November 1982, June 1983–87). Since 1991, when the Prelate of Opus Dei became a bishop, these ordinations have been carried out by the Prelate himself.

(B) *The Priestly Society of the Holy Cross.* This is an association of clergy, of the type called for by the Second Vatican Council in its decree *Presbyterorum ordinis.* The Society aims to foster holiness in the fulfilment of the priestly ministry, providing its members with ascetical and spiritual guidance to enable them to maintain, among other things, an exemplary availability and responsiveness to the requests of their bishops and to the needs of the diocese.

Priests incardinated into Opus Dei are automatically members of this Society. In addition deacons and priests already incardinated into a diocese may join the Society, in response to a vocation to live their ministry in their diocese according to the spirit of Opus Dei, while remaining entirely and exclusively dependent upon their bishop. They try to make their own the motto 'nihil sine Episcopo', and to practise fraternity especially with the other priests of the local clergy and with all priests. Among these they seek to foster priestly holiness and to encourage complete submission to the ecclesiastical hierarchy, who thus find their authority reinforced.

Lay people

(A) *Number.* In the year 2000, the lay faithful of the Prelature (divided more or less equally between the men's and women's section) numbered around 80,000. Most of them are married and live with their own families. A vocation is a personal calling, so it is often only the husband, or the wife, or one of the children, who is in Opus Dei.

(B) *Variety.* The lay members are from all social levels and occupations. The fact that there are a large number of manual and clerical workers in Opus Dei obviously does not attract the attention of some of the media, which tend to be much more interested in members who are socially more prominent. For the founder, nevertheless, 'the vocation of a railway porter is as important as that of a company director'. And the ideal of holiness proclaimed by Opus Dei in practice finds a strong response in rural as in urban areas, among the young as among the old, with academics as with the unlettered, in organised professions as in those where the type of work is determined more by circumstances and events, in westernised societies and in those steeped in Eastern, African or other traditions, in strongly Christian areas and in pagan or mission countries.

Within the same vocation to holiness and apostolate, Opus Dei unites doctors, lawyers, miners, bricklayers, artists, politicians, farmers, housewives, film directors, teachers, academics, manual workers, fishermen, small shopkeepers, industrialists, craftsmen, air pilots, research workers, nurses, members of the armed forces, cleaning ladies, taxi drivers, hairdressers, models, journalists, cattle-dealers, judges, technicians, trade union officials, railwaymen, sportsmen, philosophers, policemen, diplomats, writers . . . There is no danger of elitism because 'out of every hundred souls,' Mgr. Escrivá used to say, 'we are interested in all hundred of them'.

It is worth pointing out that, in spite of such great diversity of members, there is no difference or distinction made between men and women, single or married, priests or lay. Here, undoubtedly, is a characteristic of Opus Dei which further explains why it was erected as a personal Prelature, and the appropriateness of its place in the ordinary hierarchical and pastoral structure of the People of God.

(C) *Relationships with bishops.* The laity, following the statutes of the Prelature, depend on (or, are subject to) the bishops of the place where they live, in accordance with the norms of Canon Law, exactly like other faithful, their equals. Their dependence on the Prelate applies only to areas that refer to the specific ends of Opus Dei. The training they receive from the Prelature serves to strengthen their union with the bishop and other pastors of their local Church, because it helps them in their efforts to be exemplary Catholics.

They venerate their bishops: they show them affection and try to encourage the same feelings among other faithful. They contribute, as far as their personal circumstances permit, to carrying out the pastoral directives of the bishop of the diocese or of the episcopal conference. The same is true of their relations with their parish priests.

INCORPORATION INTO OPUS DEI

Joining Opus Dei

There is a minimum age of 18 years. There is no maximum age; people of over 80 have received a vocation. Incorporation into the Prelature of the Holy Cross and Opus Dei is brought about by a mutual and stable bond of a contractual nature between the Prelate and the lay faithful who choose to join it. (The situation of the clergy of the Prelature is the same as that of the laity, for they join Opus Dei as laymen and only receive Holy Orders later on.) To underline the secular character of this incorporation, the Declaration of the Congregation for Bishops specified that it does not have the force of a vow. The commitment of members of Opus Dei is thus radically different in its nature from that of the religious and of consecrated persons who profess the three vows of poverty, chastity and obedience. The state in life of members of Opus Dei is therefore completely unaltered by their belonging to the Prelature: the total absence of a 'sacred bond' means that each person remains an ordinary lay member of the faithful in the diocese to which he belongs.

Their link with Opus Dei is acquired by means of a formal,

contractual declaration made bilaterally in the presence of two witnesses. By this declaration:

(a) The Prelature promises to provide continual training and guidance in doctrinal, spiritual, ascetical and apostolic matters, as well as personal pastoral help from the priests of the Prelature: and to fulfil the other obligations to the faithful of the Prelature determined by the norms governing the Prelature.

(b) The member in question – the other party to the contract – freely declares that he or she is firmly resolved to seek holiness with all his or her strength, and to carry out an apostolate according to the spirit of Opus Dei. He or she promises to remain under the jurisdiction of the Prelate and of those who help him in the government of the Prelature, so as to devote himself or herself to the aims proper to it; to fulfil all the duties of his or her condition as a member of Opus Dei; to follow all the norms of the Prelature, and the indications of its authorities, in matters of government, spirit and apostolate; this he or she promises until the contract is renewed, or for the rest of his or her life, as the case may be.

Leaving Opus Dei

No one remains in the Prelature against his or her will. Everyone is there, as the founder said, 'because he feels like it, which is the most supernatural reason of all'. He made it quite clear that while a person needs to knock insistently on the door to be let in, the door is wide open to let that person leave. This is not to say that people are not helped to persevere with the appropriate spiritual guidance.

The commitments

The Declaration mentioned above states that the personal commitments of the members are 'ascetical, formational and apostolic'. These refer to the specific areas recognised by the Church, where all Catholics enjoy autonomy in their actions, and where each person can exercise his legitimate freedom and personal responsibility. These commitments bear on matters which were not previously subject to any ecclesiastical jurisdiction, precisely because they are areas where the faithful are free.

The commitments require obedience to the directors of the Prelature – an obedience which is undertaken freely, and which Mgr. Escrivá described as 'voluntary and responsible': that is to say, marked by a spirit of initiative characteristic of human beings who are 'neither stones nor corpses', but 'intelligent and free'.

(A) *The ascetical commitments* concern the carrying out of a plan of spiritual life. This is demanding, but adaptable to the personal circumstances of each member, it leads him or her progressively, 'up a gentle slope' to find God in his or her everyday work and other activities.

The plan comprises an intense sacramental life, centred on daily Mass and Holy Communion, and weekly Confession; the habitual practice of mental prayer (up to an hour a day); reading the New Testament and some spiritual book; saying the Rosary; an examination of conscience; a monthly day of recollection and yearly retreat; constant seeking of the presence of God; consideration of one's divine filiation; frequent spiritual communions; ejaculatory prayers, etc.

In addition every member should maintain a spirit of mortification and penance, including corporal mortification, according to the age, health and circumstances of each. This is in line with a practice in the Catholic Church which goes back to Christ himself, involving methods approved by the Church, and carefully avoiding all excesses.

Special importance is accorded to daily work, as a true hinge of holiness and apostolate. It is within their work that members of Opus Dei try to acquire human or natural virtues – hard work, a spirit of service, honesty, loyalty, self-sacrifice, etc., as well as supernatural virtues.

These ascetical commitments are supported by both personal and collective spiritual direction.

(B) The *formational commitments* refer to the training in religious doctrine which members of Opus Dei receive throughout their entire life, in accordance with individual possibilities and capacities.

This formation aims at nourishing the spiritual and apostolic life of each person, combining 'the piety of children with the sure doctrine of theologians', to ensure that there are people in all areas of society who are intellectually equipped to carry out an effective apostolate of spreading good doctrine in the exercise of their profession or trade.

This training, which is more concentrated during the first years of incorporation into the Prelature, is given individually or in courses for homogenous groups. The directors of the Prelature are careful to see that the time given to doctrinal classes does not cause neglect of family or professional duties.

Philosophical and theological training is given to all members as far as their personal, family and occupational circumstances permit. In accordance with the Statutes of the Prelature, this training carefully follows the Magisterium of the Church; and in conformity with the norms established by the Second Vatican Council and by the Holy See, it follows the doctrine of St Thomas Aquinas. Opus Dei has no doctrine of its own and does not form its own schools of thought on issues in philosophy, theology or canon law which are left open by the Church for free discussion.

(C) The *apostolic commitments* lead the faithful of the Prelature to exercise the common duty of all Christians to do apostolate, in a practical, constant and effective manner.

The apostolate has two aspects – firstly, bringing the doctrine of Christ to those who do not yet know it, and secondly, encouraging Christians to respond to the demands of their call to holiness in the carrying out of the duties of their state and of their everyday work.

In the spirituality of Opus Dei, the apostolic vocation is not seen as an activity to be added on to various others, or to be carried out only at certain times. Apostolate is an essential part of the Christian vocation *per se*; it follows, then, that it must be continuous and intense, an integral part of a Christian's response to all the situations that arise in everyday life.

In their dealings with their friends, colleagues and so on, members of Opus Dei carry out an apostolate of giving doctrine and dispelling ignorance. A number of them feel motivated to live apostolic celibacy so as to be entirely available, and to live an eschatological witness so essential to Christian life.

The statutes of the Prelature stress that the apostolic activities of its members should always make use of supernatural means first and foremost, and that they must moreover respect the legitimate freedom of the consciences of others.

LIFE OF THE MEMBERS

Normal Christians

To those who wished to understand the lives of members of Opus Dei, and to have a clear point of reference to start from, Mgr. Escrivá used to say that 'the simplest thing to do is to think of the lives of the early Christians', who incarnated Christianity in their lives and spread it around them with naturalness.

The life of a member is the same as that which he led before he joined the Prelature. It keeps the same family framework; it takes place in the same occupational and social setting. Mgr. Escrivá explained that 'an essential characteristic of the spirit of Opus Dei is that it does not take anyone out of his place – "unusquisque, in qua vocatione vocatus est, in ea permaneat": "everyone should remain in the state in which he was called" (1 Cor 7: 20). On the contrary, it leads everyone to carry out his task and the duties of his state as perfectly as possible.' The faithful of the Prelature are not people who live apart from the world and enter it to work as labourers, businessmen, or whatever. They *are* labourers, businessmen, or whatever, with their own professional enthusiasms and particular outlook, whose work and relationships with their friends are ways which lead to God.

To put it another way: no one, on answering his calling to Opus Dei, changes his normal way of life, his ordinary work, or his plans. That is the characteristic of Opus Dei, which has 'the strangeness of not being strange', as the founder put it.

Only a small number of celibate members live in centres of the Prelature, so as to be available for other members and managing apostolic activities, while continuing to work in their own jobs. They live a family life in the centre which has the characteristics of the lives of normal Christian families.

External behaviour

A member of Opus Dei, therefore, cannot be distinguished from his professional colleagues in any way: 'We are identical to others, not "like others"', wrote the founder in 1930, 'and we have, in common with them, their concerns as citizens, and those proper to our trade or profession, and other typical interests; the same kinds of background, the same ways of dressing and behaving.'

Being ordinary Christians, not religious, members dress like anyone else in their position, with nothing odd or eccentric about them, adapting their timetable to the demands of their activities, usually living with their families, and so on. Opus Dei does not set out to create or spread special ways of doing things – not even special acts of piety. It tries to bring its members, and those who benefit from its spirituality, to put into practice the ascetical and apostolic demands of the Christian faith. The personality of each member is not just respected, but strengthened and enriched.

The spirituality of Opus Dei lays stress on the role of the individual, in his own sanctification and in the sanctification of others. It is open to creative ideas; there are no typical activities proper to Opus Dei, no collective demonstrations, no stereotyped approaches or group behaviour.

Naturalness

Naturalness prevents members from making a show of their membership. 'It would be repugnant for them to carry a placard on their backs, saying: "Let it be known that I am committed to God's service". That would be neither lay nor secular.' On the other hand, they do not hide or disguise the fact that they belong to the Prelature. Those who know them know that they are members, for their daily life and apostolate are an open witness to it.

Openness

If personal apostolate of individual members is carried out in the open, this is even more the case with the corporate apostolates of Opus Dei, organised in or from its centres which are always officially and publicly known to be such. This way of doing apostolate does not depend on any spectacular or propagandist means. It is characterised by the naturalness that comes from realising that 'Jesus Christ has made holiness the condition for effectiveness in apostolic activity', and that their lives would make no sense if they were not characterised by prayer and an eagerness to bring souls closer to God. To work in this way grand strategies are not needed, nor will closed, regimented approaches help. Every member tries to work effectively, without drawing attention to himself, with the same naturalness with which Jesus sanctified his everyday life in Nazareth, while actually carrying out the Redemption of the human race. The members live a collective humility – which is why the work of Opus Dei is done with so little fuss.

Opus Dei works everywhere with the legal recognition and consent both of the civil and ecclesiastical authorities, the latter as foreseen in the Declaration. The names of the directors and priests, and of the apostolic activities, are public knowledge and can be found in all the relevant directories and yearbooks.

CORPORATE WORKS OF APOSTOLATE

What they are

The basic message of Opus Dei is an invitation to holiness in the middle of everyday activities. The apostolate of its own members is therefore primarily a personal 'apostolate of friendship and trust'. Nevertheless for apostolic purposes, some members of Opus Dei sometimes join forces with their friends – including people who may not be Catholics or indeed Christians – to set up 'corporate' works of apostolate. These activities are always professional and lay in character; they radiate the warmth of the Christian spirit, and also contribute to resolving problems in specific areas of education, medicine and public health, professional training, social and human development, and so on. If the managers of an activity like this so request, Opus Dei sometimes accepts responsibility for the Christian teaching and counselling given in these activities – in which case they can properly be described as 'corporate' or 'collective' apostolates of Opus Dei. This often entails a centre of Opus Dei being set up at the premises where the activity takes place, in which the members more directly involved in looking after it can live.

These corporate apostolates are always initiated and managed by ordinary citizens exercising their normal rights. They are responsible for the entire technical side of things – planning, development, and management finances; the hiring of qualified personnel; relations with the relevant civil and ecclesiastical authorities, etc. They are lay citizens doing ordinary, secular work, just like their colleagues in a similar job or trade.

As their directors are at pains to point out, these activities, despite their apostolic inspiration, are not Church activities, officially or unofficially. They are simply private initiatives, run with a lay – that is, secular – outlook. They are set up and they develop following the regulations and customs of each place, without privilege of any sort; they come under the same regulations as activities promoted by any other citizen, foundation, or association. The people who run them are directly responsible to the appropriate civil authorities.

These corporate activities are as varied as the needs and circumstances of the places in which they start. They spring up in a natural way from the needs of society, and it is society which in the end benefits most.

Characteristics

The corporate works reflect the essential characteristics of Opus Dei. They are directed above all towards a spiritual end: they are always clearly apostolic, in the fields of teaching, social services, development, and so on. They could never be industrial or commercial activities such as businesses, publishers, newspapers, or banks. Activities of the latter type could certainly constitute the personal professional work of members; but in this case they are personally responsible, and Opus Dei has no say or influence in them. The Prelature cannot take any responsibility, even indirectly, for anyone's work activities, be it designing a bridge, making a film, or selling a product.

The directors of the corporate apostolates try to help those who take part in them to develop their personalities to the full, without pressurising anyone, since 'an apostolate which did not completely respect freedom of consciences would certainly not be right'. All those who attend activities know that they can benefit, if they so wish, from the doctrinal and religious training and guidance made available to them. They learn to use their personal freedom in an upright manner (and, if they are Christians, with a supernatural sense), to respect the freedom of others, and to shoulder their own responsibilities. Thanks to this sense of freedom and responsibility, each person feels encouraged to work well and eagerly. Checking and supervision become unnecessary: each person feels at home, and all that is needed is a simple timetable.

These activities, moreover, are open to men and women of all backgrounds, without discrimination on the grounds of social status, race, religion or ideology. This openness extends not only to those attending activities, but also to managers and employees of all kinds. Non-Catholics who frequent such centres find an atmosphere of understanding, respect and friendship. In order to develop, a person needs to live with others and share experiences, and this living-together does not work unless everyone's personal freedom is respected. A natural sense of human solidarity suggests one should put personal gifts at the service of others, as otherwise they become useless. In these centres a genuine family life develops and those who get into this family life often feel motivated to come closer to Christianity, because of the witness to the faith lived by those they find there.

Financial resources

The success of Opus Dei's apostolate is based on the grace of God, and on a life of prayer, work and self-sacrifice. But financial resources are also needed. By its very nature an apostolic activity is not profitable, and in addition, many of them are intended for people with little or no resources.

There are normally four sources of finance.

(a) Each corporate activity relies firstly on its own resources: tuition or accommodation fees in the case of a school or student hall, income from the sale of produce in the case of an agricultural college, or revenue from the sale of arts and crafts. But inevitably these never cover all the costs, and often not even a small fraction of them.

(b) Members give part of what they earn from their job to support these apostolates. Each gives what he can: there is no fixed quota which would characterise different types of members, nor do individual members commit themselves to paying a fixed amount. Each looks at his own situation and, following his conscience, sees what he can give towards the upkeep of the apostolic activities having taken into account his family, professional and other responsibilities.

(c) Thirdly, and above all, there are many generous people –

including co-operators of Opus Dei – who give what they can. Some are spiritually motivated; others, who apart from the apostolic aspects, are attracted by the social dimension of these initiatives and the welfare contribution they make.

(d) Finally, these activities are often entitled to grants from government agencies, for they carry out social work that relieves the state from part of its obligations.

Examples of corporate activities

Figures given for those attending courses or graduating are those of the 1984 edition.

(A) *Technical Training Centres and Trade Schools*

(a) The *Centro ELIS* (Educazione, Lavoro, Istruzione, Sport) in the industrial Tiburtino district of Rome is run for blue-collar workers. It was started when Pope John XXIII decided to entrust a social project in this neighbourhood to members of Opus Dei. It was financed by funds collected for the eightieth birthday of Pope Pius XII. Coming in person to open the centre in 1965, Pope Paul VI declared 'Tutto, tutto qui è Opus Dei' (Everything here is Opus Dei, is the Work of God). Pope John Paul II expressed the same sentiments on his visit to ELIS in 1984.

This centre has a residence for 140 (apprentices, craftsmen, technicians, employees and young people undergoing work training). 80% of them get a remission of all or part of their accommodation fees; 10% come from Africa, the Middle East and the third world generally. The residence is organised in units of 16 or so, to keep things on a human scale and to foster a family atmosphere.

The Technical College trains 250 workers in electro-mechanical engineering, technical drawing, data processing, numerical control, etc., using its own workshops (300,000 sq. ft.). It has trained 2,200 apprentices since it began. The courses are all free, financed by the region of Latium (70%) and by the Italian Ministry for Foreign Affairs (30%). The Centre also organises courses for foreigners as part of programmes of technical aid set up by that Ministry (two-month courses in English, Spanish, or

French for foremen and training co-ordinators, and eight-month courses for instructors in mechanical and electro-mechanical engineering).

The facilities provided by the ELIS Sports Group and Sports School cover 200,000 sq ft. and give over 300 youngsters a basic grounding in different sports, particularly football and basketball. They also take part in tournaments and even international competitions.

A youth hostel (accommodating 60) welcomes groups from all over the world. Apprentices and students make use of the hostel when visiting Rome for congresses, tours, etc.

An experimental state secondary school was opened in 1980 and now has three forms and nearly 100 pupils (this number seems set to rise, given the circumstances in the Tiburtino district). ELIS Club, for boys of 10–14, fosters personal friendship and develops character and a habit of study among its members. An Information Centre and Library (5,000 volumes) promotes reading and cultural development and houses a reference collection for the professional centre. There are activities for parents, such as courses on family guidance.

Independently of these activities, the women's section of Opus Dei looks after the adjacent Scuola Alberghiera Femminile Internazionale which gives professional training in catering and domestic work. And the local parish of San Giovanni Battista has been entrusted to priests of Opus Dei.

Other activities of this type elsewhere include:
Centro de Capacitacion Obrera Kinal, Guatemala; Instituto de Desarrollo Personal, Mexico; Tajamar, Madrid; Midtown Centre, Chicago; Monteverde, Bogota; Centro Cultural y Deportivo Oeste, Buenos Aires; Centro Tecnico CETEC, Saõ Paolo.

(b) For people in rural areas there is, for example, the Instituto Rural Valle Grande, at San Vincente de Canete (Peru), a centre giving technical training in agriculture and animal husbandry. It works throughout the central mountain ranges of Peru and the corresponding coastlands – an area of about 6,000 sq. miles and up to 18,000 feet above sea level.

Since 1973, Valle Grande has greatly expanded its work by setting up *Escuelas Radiofonicas Americanas* (radio schools). It has 365 listening posts scattered among the villages, and broadcasts courses in aspects of agriculture, animal husbandry, general culture, Christian values, etc.

The Instituto Rural has an auditorium seating 200, classrooms for 600 students and a residence for 30. It fosters all-round development by means of technical training, co-operation and development, social teaching of the Church, etc. Life in the residence during the intensive courses aims to help people avoid rivalries and to nourish new friendships – so necessary in the sierra, where life is very tough.

Courses cover methods of improving farming yields, bee-keeping, family poultry farming; cattle vaccination; pruning and grafting of fruit trees; cheese-making; the use of insecticides and fertilizers. It has soil testing laboratories, provides agricultural advisory and veterinary services, and helps in community projects such as irrigation systems. In 1979 some 2,850 people working in farming received direct training, thus benefiting a population of around 13,000.

Valle Grande is financed partly by the sale of the produce of its poultry farm and bee-keeping programme, and by the services furnished by its two laboratories. This provides about 50% of the upkeep. The rest comes from Peruvian and foreign agencies for aid and rural development. Almost all the activities of the Instituto Rural are thus more or less free – only a token fee is asked for, and this so that those attending can better appreciate and value the help they are receiving. With help from the Italian government, Valle Grande has developed the Club Cultural y Deportivo Azor for boys of the area between the ages of nine and seventeen, and the Paracan Medical Post for first aid, preventive medicine and research into the diseases of the region.

Other centres along the same lines include: *Las Garzas, Chile*; *Instituto Tecnico Agrario Bell-lloc*, Gerona (Spain); *Escuela Agropecuaria el Peñon*, Morelos (Mexico); and numerous family agricultural schools.

(B) *Schools, Colleges and Third Level Educational Establishments*

(a) Schools and Youth Clubs. When it opened its doors in 1961, *Kianda Secretarial College* in Nairobi, Kenya, was the first multi-racial educational centre for women in Africa. It takes 300 pupils, studying either for a one-year secretarial diploma (typing, short-hand, commercial English, business management etc.) or for a two-year bilingual (English-French) secretarial diploma. Some 500 students have passed through Kianda since it started; almost a third of them have been foreigners from 40 countries (17 of them African). One in five receive a bursary. They generally have no trouble finding work immediately, and so can quickly help their families, of which they are often the only breadwinner (many come from a rural background and a large family). A number of Kenyan families discover Christianity and some become Christians through contact with the College.

The pupils themselves as a social service give classes in reading and writing to local people, and make visits to the sick and elderly. The teaching staff, composed mainly of past pupils, is trained at Milikiwa, a centre looked after by Kianda. Kianda has also provided the expertise to help set up *Lagoon College* in Lagos, run along similar lines.

In 1967, the *Kibondeni School* was opened, teaching hotel management and domestic science. Over 1,000 pupils have now done the two-year course for a Certificate of Institutional Management. The school has also set up a *Home Economics Club* for young girls in Nairobi, and *Watani Hostel*, which is a residence for past pupils and domestic employees. There are plans for another centre, specialising in hotel management.

Kianda Residence also dates from 1967. It has a capacity for 100, and takes students from Kianda College and other establishments. Forty per cent of the residents are from abroad; there are twenty bursaries available.

Kianda High School was started in 1977. It is a secondary school with 360 places; on average, 90 places are taken by foreign students, from 15 nations to date. The school organises a French essay competition every year, and takes part in the Kenya Music

Festival, scientific competitions, etc. Great attention is paid to involvement of parents and to further training of teachers.

At Kianda, as at other centres, days of recollection, retreats and courses in Catholic teaching are held to give pupils the opportunity of deepening their faith and making it accessible to others.

The Seido Language Institute was started in Ashiya (Japan) in 1961 by the Seido Foundation for the Advancement of Education. The Institute is used by 1,500 registered students — men and women from higher education and industry — who attend twice a week or follow intensive or sandwich courses for up to three years. The languages taught are English (by far the most popular), French, German and Spanish. Seido has developed an original method of teaching English which takes into account the particular difficulties experienced by the Japanese student. *Modern English: an oral approach* is now used by over 500 centres of education in the country. The Institute has opened a publishing division which produces textbooks, tapes from the Seido English system, a review of Catholic documents, catechisms, spiritual books, etc.

Seido Institute also has a youth club. The Seido Overseas Summer Study Abroad Program permits students to stay with families abroad while attending summer courses. The Institute which was enlarged to five floors in 1972 also houses a *Cultural Centre*, which, among other things does a lot to make the Faith better known in a country where Catholics are a tiny minority. (Of the 15,000 people who have done courses at Seido, a mere 300 were Catholics.)

Other clubs for young people include: *Club Turey*, Puerto Rico; *Tamezin Club*, London; *Ganunda Boys Club*, Montreal; *Club de Valk*, Maastricht; *Frontier Club*, Roseville (Australia); *Club Montelar*, Madrid; *Clube Xenon*, Lisbon; *Centre d'Etudes pour la femme*, Brussels; *Colegio Los Pinos*, Quito; *Greygarth Boys Club*, Manchester; *Club Juvenil Yalam*, Hermosillo (Mexico); *Kelston Club*, London; *Anchor Youth Club*, Dublin. Examples of schools and colleges are *Strathmore College*, Nairobi; *Gaztelueta*, Bilbao; *The Heights*, Washington and *Viaro*, Barcelona.

Examples of non-residential education and cultural centres are: *Dunreath*, Glasgow; *Ely University Centre*, Dublin; *Glenalvon*, Glasgow.

(b) Student halls of residence. One of the seven Colleges on the campus of the University of New South Wales is *Warrane College*. Opened in 1970, it was the first Australian college to be run by Catholic university lecturers as a professional job. Three-quarters of the construction costs were met by the State of New South Wales; the rest came from private funds. Over 2,000 students from 33 countries have passed through Warrane. A third of the students receive scholarships, mainly from the State.

Warrane has its own traditions and style. An example is its 'orientation week' at the start of each new academic year, for residents from different countries in Asia and Oceania. Final year students help run this programme of introduction to life at Warrane and at the university in general. There are also sporting traditions such as the election of the 'Sportsman of the Week' — the one out of 200 students who is adjudged to have best defended Warrane's colours in inter-college competitions in any of twenty sports.

Most of the activities at Warrane are aimed at complementing studies followed at university. There is a programme of tutorials in more than thirty subjects. There is also a programme of professional orientation, centred on job opportunities. Many residents and non-residents (including non-Catholics) take part in activities of a spiritual nature. The college takes catechism classes in local schools, and organises visits to the old and the sick.

The cultural life of Warrane springs from the initiatives of the residents — talks, debates, musical get-togethers, cultural activities, excursions, films, and shows on residents' birthdays. Recently summer courses have begun on computer studies, English language courses and other programmes for foreigners, for example from New Caledonia.

Other halls of residence include: *Ashwell House*, London; *Studentenheim Während*, Vienna; *Centro Cultural Piñeda*, Barcelona; *Centro Universitario Cuidad Vieja*, Guatemala; *Layton Study Centre*,

Brookfield (USA); *Colegio Mayor Alcor*, Madrid; *Imoran Study Centre*, Lagos; *Résidence Universitaire Steenberg*, Louvain; *Studentenheim Schweidt*, Cologne; *Centro Estudiantil Miravalles*, San Jose (Costa Rica); *Grandpont House*, Oxford; *Centro Universitario Montefaro*, Montevideo; *Greygarth Hall*, Manchester; *Tanglaw University Center*, Manila; *Residenza Universitario Internazionale*, Rome; *Centro Universitario Monteavila*, Caracas; *Residencia y Centro Cultural Alborada*, Santiago (Chile); *Riverview*, Montreal; *Centro de Estudiantes Los Esteros*, Guayaquil (Equador); *Nullamore University Residence*, Dublin; *Residencia Universitaria Feminina Inaya*, Bogota; *Studentenheim Fluntern*, Zurich; *Netherhall House*, London; *Glenard University Residence*, Dublin.

(c) Universities. The University of Navarre was founded in Pamplona in 1952. It has faculties of law, medicine, philosophy and arts, pharmacology, science, canon law, theology, information sciences, and economics; in addition it has schools of architecture, industrial engineering, librarianship, nursing, laboratory assistantship, institutes of pedagogy, liberal arts, Spanish language and culture, and languages; and at San Sebastian, a school of engineering and an institute of secretarial administration. It has eight university halls of residence with a total capacity of 800 run by the university.

Since its inception about 22,000 students have done courses at the University of Navarre. In the academic year 1985–86 there were 12,640 registered students, 568 of whom were foreigners from 39 different countries, plus some 6,700 taking part in proficiency programmes and in-service training. More than 4,000 students received scholarships or grants from the University. These are given, with the aid of the association of Friends of the University of Navarre, mainly to students from the Navarre region (70%). The Spanish State gives 850 scholarships.

The financing of the University for the academic year 1985–86 was as follows: enrolment fees 77.92%; private assistance and research funding 19.79%; regional institutions 1.20%; the State 0.03%; other 1.06%.

There are numerous cultural activities: conferences, sports

championships, exhibitions, photographic and poetry competitions, dramatic productions and musical activities. All the centres in the University run activities of a cultural and spiritual nature – theology courses, series of conferences, seminars, talks, etc. – to complement the other studies of the students. The Chaplaincy, for its part, organises retreats, Easter conferences, meditations, a Novena to the Immaculate Conception, Marian activities during the month of May, and so on. These take place in the oratories of some of the faculties, for the teaching staff, the students (and their families) and the non-teaching personnel.

The University Hospital comes under the Faculty of Medicine. It has 500 beds and in 1985 some 9,292 patients were admitted and over 54,000 outpatient cases dealt with.

The *Instituto de Estudios Superiores de la Empresa* (IESE) – Institute for the Third Level Business Studies – also part of the University of Navarre, has been in operation in Barcelona since 1958. It runs courses in Management and MBA degree courses in Economics and Business Management. Working in collaboration with Harvard, IESE has acquired an international reputation. At present there are students from 34 countries studying there, and some 740 graduated in the academic year 1985–86. Over 8,000 in total have attended courses there to date.

In October 1984, the *Centro Academico Romano della Santa Croce* was opened in Rome. Dependent on the University of Navarre, it has faculties of theology and canon law.

The University Library has over 400,000 titles. *Ediciones Universidad de Navarre* (EUNSA) – Navarre University Press – published 90 titles in the academic year 1985–86: 65 books and 25 issues of nine specialized reviews (*Nuestro Tiempo, Revista de Medicina, Scripta Theologica, Ius Canonicum, Persona y Derecho, Anuario Filosofico, Anuario de Derecho Internacional, Exerpta et Dissertationibus in Iure Canonico,* and *Exerpta et Dissertationibus in Sacra Theologia*).

Various activities are run by the university over the summer months: refresher courses for graduates, summer courses for medical students, intensive courses in Spanish language and culture, philosophy conferences, seminars on practical applications of Canon Law, etc.

There are two other universities similar to the University of Navarre: University of Piura, Peru and La Sabana University, Colombia.

(C) *Conference Centres and Catering Schools.* In 1952, an old hacienda dating from colonial times became *Montefalco Conference Centre* (Morelos State, Mexico). Made up of three main buildings, it can now house 110 people at a time, in separate groups – housewives, students, professionals, domestic employees, secretaries, manual workers, etc. – 5,000 people a year in all, and more than 50,000 since the centre was started. The activities (cultural and study courses, professional training programmes, sports activities, retreats, etc.) are organised by other corporate works of Opus Dei in Mexico.

In 1956, the *Centro de Estudios Montefalco* was added. This offers a two-year training course in catering and domestic work. The 40 students each receive a half scholarship, sponsored by a promoters' association, and cover the rest of their expenses by the work they do. They also give training courses in many villages of the region.

The students of the Study Centre also help as tutors in the *Escuela Feminina de Montefalco*, which opened its doors in 1958. In 1969 this rural school set up the *Telesecundiaria* (a three year secondary school course also broadcast on television), with 192 pupils attending; and, in 1978, a teacher training school (a four-year course, with 135 students). Almost 2,700 pupils have passed through the girls' school. Enrolment fees are very low: the school survives on monthly grants from a sponsorship association. Besides professional training and religious guidance, special attention is given to character development, personal and domestic hygiene, care of food and clothes, deportment, temperance, a sense of responsibility, a spirit of hard work, and so on. The school takes part in activities at the community, state and national levels: sports competitions, conferences, exhibitions on literature, physics, chemistry, social science and so on. In addition, as a service to the rural communities of the Amilpas Valley, it organises activities of a social, cultural or spiritual nature in about twenty villages of the valley.

Club Tonameyo is attended by 140 young girls from the surrounding villages. They learn music, crafts, home economics, cooking and dressmaking. They go on excursions and courses, and they receive talks on character and spiritual development. About 500 young children are being prepared for their first Holy Communion.

Similar centres include: *Lakefield Catering and Educational Centre*, London, opened by the Queen Mother in 1966; *Crannton Catering Centre*, Dublin; *Ecole technique d'hotellerie Dosnon*, near Rheims (France); *L'Essor, Centre de Formation pour la Femme*, Montreal; *Punlaan School*, Manila; *Mikawa Cooking School*, Nagasaki; *Escuela Tecnica de Formacion Profesional Besana*, Madrid; *Kenvale Training Centre*, Sydney; *Lexington Institute*, Chicago; *Instituto de Capacitacion Integral en Estudios domesticos*, Buenos Aires; *Houswirthschaftliche Ausbildungsstätte Müngersdof*, Cologne; *Wickenden Manor*, Sussex (England); *Lismullin Conference Centre*, Tara (Ireland); *Makiling Conference Center*, Manila; *Shelbourne Conference Center*, Valparaiso (USA); *Thornycroft Hall*, Macclesfield (England); *Ballyglunin Park Conference Centre*, Tuam (Ireland); *Castello di Urio*, Lake Como (Italy); *Kimlea*, Tigoni (Kenya); *Iroto Conference Centre*, Nigeria.

Further information on apostolic activities of Opus Die can readily be obtained from the information office in the corresponding country. For example: 5 Orme Court, London W2 4RL (London 221-9176); 9 Hume Street, Dublin 2 (Dublin 614949); 330 Riverside Drive, New York, NY 10025 (914-235-1201).

The corporate apostolates of the Prelature of Opus Dei must be carefully distinguished from many other cultural and formative activities which are also promoted and looked after by members of Opus Dei, but for which the Prelature assumes no responsibility. These are personal initiatives of members (either alone or with friends and colleagues) which normally constitute their professional work. Here the responsibility for the moral and doctrinal orientation, as well as the purely technical aspects, does not in any way rest with the Prelature but wholly and entirely with the promoters of the activity.

5: Other Aspects of Its Spirituality

THE WRITINGS OF MGR. ESCRIVÁ

The founder of Opus Dei was a prolific writer. 'My name is Escriva,' he used to joke, 'and I write a lot' – playing on the Spanish verb 'escribir', to write.

He had undoubted literary talent. His writings in the original Spanish show precision and vigour. The style is unpretentious and avoids an over-easy appeal to the emotions. It employs a rich vocabulary and a use of imagery at times reminiscent of the gospel parables.

A feature which runs through almost everything he wrote is the way he takes as a starting point something from Scripture either the New or Old Testament. He meditated upon God's Word so as to 'get inside the scenes of the Holy Gospels, to be just one more person among those present', Mgr. Alvaro del Portillo has written. In this way, Mgr. Escrivá brings out fresh insights and draws practical lessons, directly relevant to everyday life, and accessible to every reader. His writings are also notable for their frequent quotations from the Fathers of the Church. Most of his published works include an index of references to Scripture, the Fathers and Doctors of the Church and to the documents of the Magisterium, in addition to a subject index.

Published Work

(A) *The Way* has been published in 192 editions, in 42 languages, with a total run of more than 4,000,000 copies. Apart from the main European languages, *The Way* has also been published for example in Arabic, Armenian, Basque, Catalan, Croatian, Danish, Finnish, Irish, Greek, Hebrew, Hungarian, Japanese,

Lithuanian, Maltese, Polish, Quechua, Rumanian, Tagalog and Czech. There are also some Braille editions in different languages.

The Way was first published in Cuenca in February 1934 under the title Consideraciones espirituales. It acquired its present form with one or two additions in its second edition, published in Valencia in 1939.

The book contains 999 points – this three digit multiple of three being chosen in honour of the Blessed Trinity. A number of the points come from letters written or received by the author; some are advice he gave to people; some come from things said by people who came to him for spiritual guidance; others spring from considerations he had formed in his prayer or when reading the Scriptures or other books. So The Way was firmly rooted in the interior life and pastoral activity of its author.

With its often conversational style, it puts forward a vision of Christianity which is the opposite to easy-going. Its appeal is directly to the heart of each reader.

The first of the forty-six chapters deals with character, with the human personality itself and the determination a Christian must have if he or she is to take life seriously, with the help of spiritual direction which, in turn, becomes the theme for the second chapter. As the author encourages the reader along the path of prayer (Chapter 3), he brings out the various facets of Christian and human life as they present themselves in the ordinary occurrences of every day – presence of God, interior life, the goal of sanctity, interior struggle, spiritual childhood, the cultivation of virtues, attention to little things. The chapters of The Way trace out a journey of faith that culminates in the final pages, where the life of the ordinary Christian is presented as the life of a child of God who knows he is called to take part in the mission of Christ – 'life of childhood', 'calling', 'the apostle', 'the apostolate', 'perseverance'.

'Mgr. Escrivá de Balaguer has written more than a masterpiece' (L'Osservatore Romano). Interestingly enough, The Way has been described as 'The Imitation of Christ of modern times'. The book's wide sales mean that it is playing a major role in establishing an appreciation of the supernatural value of temporal realities, and in the formation of lay people and the development of a lay spirituality.

The latest English editions are published by Four Courts Press (Dublin) and Scepter (London and New York).

(B) *Holy Rosary*: first edition, 1934; since then over 700,000 copies have been produced in 65 editions and in 23 languages. This book is basically a meditation on the fifteen joyful, sorrowful and glorious mysteries of the Rosary, and concludes with some considerations on the Litany of our Lady. The author wrote it in one session, during his thanksgiving after Mass. The book is designed to help the reader share the joys and sorrows of his fellow men, to turn with simplicity and confidence to Mary and through her to the Blessed Trinity. 'The beginning of the way, at the end of which you will find yourself completely carried away by love for Jesus, is a trusting love for Mary' (Prologue).

(C) *Conversations with Mgr. Escrivá de Balaguer*: first edition, 1968; upwards of 350,000 copies in 32 editions have been published in 9 languages. This book is a collection of seven interviews given in the sixties to *Le Figaro*, the *New York Times*, *Time*, *L'Osservatore della Domenica* and other magazines.

In it Mgr. Escrivá replies at length to questions by journalists, sometimes put quite bluntly, about the spirit of Opus Dei, about the Church (the Second Vatican Council had just ended), and about respect for the rights and freedom of the individual. He also answers questions about the idea of a university, and about the role of women in society and in the life of the Church.

Conversations finishes with a homily entitled 'Passionately loving the world', delivered in 1967 on the campus of the University of Navarre before a congregation of more than 30,000 people. The homily, notable for its profound spirituality, sums up Mgr. Escrivá's responses to the kind of questions raised in the earlier part of the book; by going to the very heart of the matter, he makes clear the spirit underlying his answers throughout the various interviews. Here he says, for instance: 'Authentic Christianity, which professes the resurrection of all flesh, has always quite logically opposed dis-incarnation, without fear of being judged materialistic. We can, therefore, rightly speak of a Christian materialism, which is boldly opposed to those forms of materialism which are blind to the spirit.'

The most recent English edition is published by Sinag Tala (Manila).

(D) *Christ is Passing By*: first edition, 1973; 44 later editions amounting to 450,000 copies in 13 languages. This book contains homilies given between 1951 and 1971 on eighteen different feast days and arranged according to the cycle of the liturgical year.

It is a stimulating and profound exposition of doctrine and of the Christian way of life. The underlying theme of divine filiation leads to the universal call to holiness, the sanctification of ordinary work, the dignity of secular life, contemplation in the middle of the world, unity of life, etc.

The English edition, first published in 1974, is currently published by Four Courts Press (Dublin) and Scepter (London and New York).

(E) *Friends of God*: first edition, 1977; 400,000 copies in 27 editions in 13 languages. This collection of homilies was the first posthumous work of Mgr. Escrivá. It consists of eighteen homilies, given between 1941 and 1968, and brought together with the aim of helping people to live in 'the friendship of God', a God who is close to the reader. This time it is the virtues which form the framework of the book.

Addressing himself to lay people who are seeking sanctity according to a specific vocation in ordinary life, Mgr. Escrivá proposes an interior life based upon humility, on presence of God, on self-denial, on turning work into prayer, on holy purity, and on a whole series of virtues which enrich the soul of the believer and help him to reach sanctity, while encouraging others to do likewise.

In the foreword, Mgr. del Portillo points out that it is not 'a theoretical treatise, nor potted hints for acquiring spiritual good manners. The homilies contain living doctrine and combine a theologian's depth with the evangelical clarity of a good shepherd of souls . . . They provide, therefore, a lesson in doctrine and in Christian life in which God is not only spoken of but spoken to.'

The first English edition was published in 1981.

(F) *The Way of the Cross*: Since the first edition in 1981, there have been 400,000 copies printed, with 18 editions in 18 languages. Alongside the traditional representation of the fourteen stations which make up the Way of the Cross five points for meditation taken from the preaching of Mgr. Escrivá have been added to each station. Words from the Gospel and from the Prophets are constantly introduced and are beautifully incorporated into the text.

It goes further than being an aid for the devout practice of the Way of the Cross. Following closely the Passion of our Lord, the book offers abundant material for meditation and for contemplative life, by pursuing paths taken by Mgr. Escrivá himself throughout his life 'which led him to the highest peaks of spiritual life.' (A. del Portillo, foreword).

The first English edition was published in 1983.

(G) *Homilies*: The homilies which have been gathered together in the two books already mentioned, as well as other homilies – on the Church, the priesthood, etc. – have been published singly as booklets. Worldwide publications have reached well over two million copies with 594 editions in 10 languages.

(H) *La Abadesa de las Huelgas*: a theological and legal monograph published in 1944 and re-issued in 1974. A penetrating study of an extraordinary case of quasi-episcopal jurisdiction exercised by the abbess of the famous convent of Las Huelgas (1187–1874) near Burgos (Spain). This book has not been published in English.

(I) *Furrow* and *The Forge*: Both these works were published posthumously, the first edition in English of *Furrow* appearing in 1987, and of *The Forge* in 1988. Like *The Way* they are collections of points intended to encourage personal prayer, and to make it easier.

Unpublished writings

There is still a great deal of unpublished material. There are letters and other documents addressed to the members of Opus Dei to help them in their apostolic work and interior lives. There are also thousands of extant letters of the founder to people of all kinds, with whom he carried out a true 'letter apostolate' throughout his life. Mgr. Escrivá's works also include a large number of homilies and talks he gave to members of Opus Dei or others.

Films

Special mention should also be made of other more recent and also unpublished material: films which were taken during the get-togethers of catechetical instructions given in the later years of the founder's life. These are particularly valuable because they give people who never met Mgr. Escrivá the opportunity to see him 'live', very much as he was.

MAIN FEATURES OF THE SPIRIT OF OPUS DEI

A study of the various writings of the founder brings out other aspects of the spirit of Opus Dei which, although belonging to the common patrimony of the Church, nevertheless have a particular flavour, and throw a special light on the secular presence in the midst of the world, a presence which is both active and contemplative.

Divine filiation

The entire teaching of Mgr. Escrivá is marked by one very profound conviction – that man is a child of God. He himself experienced this very vividly one day in the summer of 1931 on a tram in Madrid. He was asking himself how he could carry out the mission God had given him three years earlier, and there and then received a very clear reply which was to remain engraved in fire upon his soul. It was in the form of words from Psalm 2: 'You are my son, this day have I begotten you.' His soul was overwhelmed with joy and he was unable to stop himself repeating out loud, 'Abba, Pater, Abba, Pater! Abba! Abba! Abba!', calling God 'Daddy', like a child.

Later he was to write: 'Divine filiation [the fact of being a son or daughter of God] is a joyful truth, a consoling mystery. It permeates the whole of our spiritual lives, because it teaches us to come very close to our Father in heaven, to know him and to love him; it fills our interior struggle with hope and confers on us the trusting simplicity of little children. But more than this: precisely because we are sons and daughters of God, this trust also enables us to contemplate, full of love and wonder, everything that comes from the hands of God, Father and Creator. We are indeed contemplatives in the midst of the world, living the world.'

Divine filiation thus becomes the foundation of the spirituality of Opus Dei, so that when Mgr. Escrivá speaks of faith, he speaks of the faith of children of God; when he speaks of strength he is talking about the strength of children of God; if he refers to conversion, he is thinking of children of God turning back to their Father; and so on.

Devotion to our Lady

Mgr. Escrivá had great devotion to the Holy Family of Nazareth, whom he described as the 'trinity on earth'. He saw the Holy Family as the path towards union with the Blessed Trinity: St Joseph takes us to Mary; Mary leads us to Jesus, who in turn enables us to rise up towards the Father and the Holy Spirit.

The founder saw St Joseph, patron of the Church and patron of workers, as the patron of the 'Work of God'. He vigorously emphasised the key role the Patriarch played in the Holy Family. St Joseph is 'master of the interior life, since he teaches us to get to know Jesus and to live with him, and helps us realise that we belong to the family of God. St Joseph teaches us all this by being what he was – an ordinary man, the teacher of a family, a working man, who had to earn his bread by the sweat of his brow.'

Close to Joseph we find Mary, his wife. If there is one single characteristic which dominated the whole personality of Mgr. Escrivá it was his love for our Lady. His entire life and the whole story of Opus Dei has been marked by the interventions of the Mother of God and Mother of men. Convinced that 'Jesus can refuse nothing to Mary, nor to us who are children of the selfsame Mother', he invited people to 'put Mary into everything and for everything' and go through her to get to Jesus, or to return to him.

In Mary, he identified also a woman who led a life similar to that of thousands of other women, like them busy with family chores and the task of bringing up children. 'Mary sanctifies all these things down to the very smallest details, down to the sort of things which many people wrongly consider unimportant and without value: everyday work, dealings with people who love one another, the conversations and visits made between relatives and friends . . . Blessed be an ordinary life, which can be so filled with love of God!'

Unity of life

Being a Christian does not mean having a title to be proud of; it implies that we should be salt and light for all men (the call to the apostolate). This is not something peripheral; it comes to us through baptism, and helps us to act as God desires (the call to sanctity). It means that we should act, not merely out of ambition, or even for nobler aims such as philanthropy or compassion, but in order 'to reflect to the deepest and most radical level the love which Jesus Christ has shown towards us' (freedom and responsibility).

It would not be right to reduce Christianity to a set of practices or acts of piety 'without seeing its connection with ordinary life and with the sense of urgency we ought to feel as we respond to the needs of others, and as we try to right the various forms of injustice'.

Therefore, the Christian who tries to be consistent with his faith cannot be living a double life; living some of the time a life of faith with a certain set of practices, and then a pagan life for the rest of the time, in work, recreation, etc. He has to reach a 'unity of life, pure and simple', which makes him an 'all-round' Christian. He is then for example able to face social problems in a professional way, avoiding an improvised, amateur approach, and through inner conversion he will have an influence on social structures and, if he feels it necessary, work to reform them. It is in this spirit that Mgr. Escrivá promoted and encouraged a thorough education of even the most needy, as it equips them to shape their own social progress, and so ensure that their personal dignity is fully respected. 'It is in our own efforts to be better, to live a love that wishes to be pure, to control our selfishness, to give ourselves completely to others and make of our lives a constant service' that Christ manifests himself in us and we attain contemplation. Eventually it becomes impossible to distinguish 'where prayer finishes and work begins, because our work is also prayer, contemplation'.

The Mass

Continual awareness of the presence of God in the midst of ordinary activities comes about above all through participation in the holy Sacrifice of the Mass, considered not only as the non-bloody renewal of the Sacrifice of Christ on Calvary, but also as the action of each baptised person who is closely united to his Redeemer. The Christian's 'priestly soul' derives from the common priesthood of all the faithful, which is a participation in the priesthood of Christ and is essentially different from the ministerial priesthood of priests. It urges Christians to make their entire lives a continual praise of God 'so that our lives are a continuation of the previous Mass and a preparation for the following' – a Mass 'which lasts twenty-four hours'.

The Mass thus becomes 'the centre and root of the interior life', an expression taken up by the Second Vatican Council, which shows that one's entire life ought to become a true sacrifice in order to reach full identification with Christ. The Mass provides the divine energy to power one's work, one's sanctity, and one's apostolate.

Members of Opus Dei endeavour to combine this 'priestly soul' with a lay outlook: 'It is with a fully lay mentality that you exercise this priestly spirit as you offer to God your work, your rest, the joys and setbacks of the day, the holocaust of your bodies exhausted by the effort of constant service', with souls always turned towards the tabernacle, that 'prison of love', where Jesus has been 'waiting for us for twenty centuries'.

Prayer

Prayer is the only weapon, the most powerful means, to conquer in the battles of the interior life. Without it, nothing can be achieved.

Mgr. Escrivá wanted it to be 'the true prayer of the children of God and not the chatter of hypocrites': that is, to be a conversation full of love and simplicity in the presence of God who is in the centre of the soul. 'The children of God have no need of a conventional or set method in order to turn to their Father.' Here once again we have an echo of that 'Long live freedom!' which recurred so frequently in his words. 'Love is inventive, ingenious; if we are in love we will know how to discover personal, intimate paths which will lead us to continual dialogue with our Lord.'

At times prayer makes use of acts of love, ejaculatory prayers, passages from the Gospels. One needs to 'get to know' Christ in the Bread and in the Word, in the Eucharist and in prayer, Mgr. Escrivá used to emphasise. 'And we need to get to know him as we would get to know a friend, a real living person; that is what Christ is, for he has arisen again.' His primary concern was to be faithfully punctual to his fixed appointment to meet this Friend in prayer. It was an appointment arranged out of love, and Christ should not be kept waiting.

Mgr. Escrivá saw mortification as the prayer of the body. Mortification and penance were indispensable if one was to act in an upright way; they form the 'salt of our life'; without them it is impossible to be a soul of prayer. He invited people to have the following order of values in their lives. 'First, prayer; then, atonement; in the third place, very much in third place, action.'

Although he himself practised very exacting mortification, Mgr. Escrivá used to teach that the best mortification of all was to be found in the little things of each day, being careful not to mortify other people.

'You are not mortified,' he wrote, 'if you are touchy, if you listen only to the voice of your own self-centredness, if you impose your views on others, if you are not able to deprive yourself of what is superfluous and at times even of what is necessary, if you get downhearted when things do not turn out as you expected. On the other hand, you are mortified when you are able to make of yourself "all things to all men, in order to gain all".'

He used to give a whole series of other practical examples: to fulfil exactly the timetable you have set yourself; not to leave more difficult tasks for later without good reason; to find time for all the things one has to do; to treat others with the greatest charity, beginning with those closest to us; to answer patiently people who are boring or tiresome; cheerfully to take care of those who are sick or distressed; to interrupt and change our plans if the good of others requires it; to endure with good humour the thousand small upsets of each day; to finish off properly any work we have undertaken, even if the initial enthusiasm has disappeared; not to be attached to our own plans; to reprimand and correct when necessary, as the matter requires and in line with the circumstances of the person who needs to be helped in this way, etc.

He also encouraged people to practise interior mortification, 'so our conversations do not revolve around ourselves, so that we always receive unpleasant things with a smile (which can often be the best proof of a spirit of mortification), so that we make life pleasant for those around us'.

Following their founder, members of Opus Dei cultivate a spirit of mortification to purify themselves and to obtain genuine and lasting spiritual progress; to pave the way for the apostolate so it will lead to good, and to show by deeds their love for Christ who delivered himself up to death upon the Cross out of love for men. Mortification thus becomes something joyful; the interior struggle is seen as a 'smiling asceticism' since self-denial leads us to the Cross, where we find Christ with his arms open wide, ready to welcome all men: 'If you are looking for Christ what greater guarantee can you want than the Cross, to know that you have found him?' When the Cross is seen not so much as an instrument of torture but as a 'throne of triumph' upon which the Redeemer won the victory over death, sin and the devil, the whole horizon changes completely: 'Isn't it true,' asks Mgr. Escrivá, 'that when you stop being afraid of the Cross, or what people call the cross, and your will is determined to accept the will of God, you are happy, and all your worries and sufferings, physical as well as moral, disappear?'

The hidden life

The spirit of Opus Dei also aims to imitate the thirty years of hidden life of our Lord, in which the sacred humanity of Christ is made manifest, years which are part of the redemptive process and which take almost the entire life of Jesus on earth. Because there is little mention of these years in the Gospels, it might appear at first sight that they are of minor importance. However, Mgr. Escrivá shows that 'they were years of intense work and prayer; Jesus Christ lived an ordinary existence, similar to ours if you like, which was both divine and human'. By this he means that nothing in a Christian's life is useless or unimportant. Certainly life in Bethlehem or in Nazareth would have been full of the typical little jobs of home life, but if everything is for love, 'there will be no little things: everything will be big. Perseverance in little things for Love is heroism.'

Jesus is seen to be subject to Mary and Joseph, who are two creatures, certainly most perfect, but creatures nonetheless and absolutely inferior to him. The Christian obedience which Mgr. Escrivá sees modelled here led him to write, 'To obey is to be a martyr without dying.'

Humility is a precondition for obedience. God's greatness lies hidden in a stable, wrapped in swaddling clothes. God humbles himself so that we might draw close to him ... 'so that our freedom gives way not only before the sight of his power, but also before the marvel of his humility'. Thus humility becomes the touchstone of the interior life, from which one learns a little about oneself and realises that often one is no more than a rebellious instrument in the hands of God.

The hidden life of Jesus was also marked by poverty. Mgr. Escrivá outlined the characteristics of this virtue for people who remain in the world and have to make use of material goods; he invites his sons and daughters to take as a standard 'the father of a poor and large family', and taught them that 'rather than in not having, true poverty consists in being detached, in voluntarily renouncing one's dominion over things.' He also pointed out that poverty should not be confused with scruffiness or bad taste, taking also in that regard the example from our Lord: 'Our Saviour wore a seamless tunic, he ate and drank like other people ... and everyone knew that he had earned his living for many years by manual work ... In short I would say to you that we ought to wear clean clothes, be clean in body, and above all, in soul.'

Virtues

The soul who has encountered God should try to practise all virtues. At baptism it has received the theological virtues, which only God can develop within the soul: 'Lord, increase my faith, my hope and my charity!' the founder often used to say.

(a) Charity is the first of the virtues: it constitutes the essence of sanctity, since God is pure Love. 'We have to drown evil in an abundance of good' by being concerned about the good of others and above all about the good of their souls, through apostolate. Charity brings with it love of freedom, understanding, forgiveness, willingness to find excuses for others, love for the defects of others (at least to the extent that they are not an offence against God), not judging others, considering oneself the enemy of absolutely no one. 'I didn't have to learn to forgive, because our Lord taught me to love,' he told his sons and daughters. Some of them, who had been on the receiving end of strong opposition and attacks, wrote to him, saying, 'Father, no need to worry: there is not even the slightest thought against charity amongst the lot of us.' He advised some students who were imprisoned during the Spanish Civil War to play football with the anarchist prisoners so as not to bring political division into sport and also to give them a chance to learn some Christian doctrine.

Charity goes beyond justice: learning that a certain man who resembled him had been hanged in his stead in front of his mother's house, Mgr. Escrivá from that moment on never forgot to pray for him in his Mass. 'We have to behave in such a way that other people when they see us can say: That person is a Christian because there is no hatred in him, because he is understanding, because he is not a fanatic, because he controls his passions, because he is self-sacrificing, because he is peace-loving, and because he loves.'

This genuine love calls for the practice of fraternal correction, which has all the 'flavour of primitive Christianity'; by it one helps others overcome their deficiencies or one deals with situations which might otherwise undermine social harmony.

(b) Faith disposes the mind to say 'yes' to Christ, to renew constantly the unconditioned *Fiat* (Let it be done) which Mary spoke to the archangel Gabriel. 'It is all a matter of faith,' the founder used to say in every situation, whether good or seemingly terrible, because 'omnia in bonum', 'everything works out for the good'; we must accept everything as coming from the hands of our Lord Jesus Christ. Mgr. Escrivá received from God a faith 'so thick you could cut it with a knife', he used to say. He had the faith to be able to speak about the future of Opus Dei over the centuries, and to speak with conviction at a time when everything was still just beginning. At the end of the first study circle for students, in January 1933, he saw 'three thousand of them, three hundred thousand, three million ... white, black, copper-coloured, yellow, of all languages and from every latitude ...'

(c) Hope consists in the certitude that life has a meaning that transcends the boundaries of the world, and that everything – the tiniest sacrifice, the smallest act of love – can possess a value for all eternity: 'in spite of everything' – in other words, in spite of human meanness and human weakness. 'Forget that despair produced by the realisation of your weakness. True: financially you are a zero, in social standing another zero, and another in virtues, and another in talent. But to the left of those noughts stands Christ. And what an incalculable figure we get!'

Part of the virtue of hope is expectation of heaven. Towards the end of his life, when he was suffering from a cataract in both eyes, Mgr. Escrivá used to say, '*Vultum tuum, domine, requiram!* I will seek your face, O Lord. I like very much to close my eyes and think that there will come a moment, when God so wishes, when I will be able to see him, not as through a glass, darkly ... but face to face. Yes, my sons and daughters, my heart thirsts for God, the living God. When shall I see him face to face?'

He did not however as a consequence neglect his responsibilities; indeed, he had always said that he wanted to die very old, 'squeezed out like a lemon' (that is, having worked until he could give no more).

Faith, hope and charity, along with the other virtues which the grace of God brings with it, move a Christian to nurture the qualities which he shares with many others, since these 'human virtues lie at the basis of the supernatural virtues'. It would be impossible to list them all but among them are some which have a special impact in the life of an ordinary Christian living in the world: hard work, loyalty, simplicity, naturalness, sincerity, temperance, moral courage ... We might pause to consider purity or chastity, virtues which have often been caricatured and reduced to a series of taboos and prohibitions. Mgr. Escrivá saw purity as 'a joyful affirmation'; a voluntary commitment of love which does not simply aim at avoiding falls or dangerous situations, but rather, of steering away from danger as soon as one feels the first stirrings of passion, 'and even earlier'. Suggesting that for a normal person 'the question of sex comes in fourth or fifth place', Mgr. Escrivá added: 'Get used to pitching your struggle very far from the main walls of the castle'. And he used to issue the invitation to undertake 'a crusade of manliness and purity to counteract and undo the savage work of those who think that man is a beast'.

Putting these and so many other virtues into practice leads to 'peace and joy' he affirmed. Joy was the Christian's hallmark – not the 'physiological "joy" of a healthy animal' but a joy which comes from the self-denial and self surrender proper to children of God 'a joy that cannot be taken away by anyone or anything because it has its roots in the shape of a cross'.

This explains the unwaveringly positive approach of Mgr. Escrivá. He was always reminding members of Opus Dei that they should be 'sowers of peace and joy' along all the paths of the earth. 'Our Christian life must be inspired by optimism, by joy and by the firm conviction that our Lord wishes to count on us'. He went further and said that Christian optimism is not a vacuous, cheery optimism, nor a blithe human expectation that everything will work out well. 'It is an optimism which finds its deepest roots in an awareness of our freedom and in faith in divine grace; it is an optimism which leads us to be very demanding on ourselves and to make a real effort to respond to the call of God.'

The Church and the Pope

'Christ, Mary, the Pope. Have we not indicated in these three words the loves which sum up our entire Catholic faith?' Mgr. Escrivá wrote in 1934.

When he arrived for the first time in Rome and was living in an apartment from which it was possible to see the light in the window of the office where Pius XII was working, Mgr. Escrivá spent the entire night in prayer for the Pope, to whom he felt so close. Successive popes were aware of and acknowledged this affection, which was backed up by prayer and sacrifice, and Paul VI in a handwritten letter to the founder spoke of the 'fervent love of the Church and for its visible head which characterizes' Opus Dei.

The founder's veneration for Christ's Vicar led him to ask insistently for prayers for the Pope – 'whoever he may be'; it was the reason for his coming to live in Rome and for opening international educational centres there, in order to 'romanise' his sons and daughters and the whole of Opus Dei. In this way it would manifest its universality, already present in its foundational charism.

'What joy to be able to say with my whole soul: I love my Mother, the holy Church!' Many people who came close to Mgr. Escrivá confirm that he lived out this profound conviction to its ultimate consequences, to the point of offering his life as a sacrifice, that our Lord might bring to an end the trials which the Church in our time has been going through. There was one fundamental principle he inculcated in his sons and daughters: 'Serve the Church as she wants to be served', being always very united to the bishops in communion with the Apostolic See. He reacted against those who criticised the Church, especially if they were in some measure responsible for what they saw fit to criticise – because they were guilty of the serious injustice of 'making the wretchedness of some of the children appear to be faults of the Mother'.

MARRIAGE AS A CHRISTIAN VOCATION

The dignity of marriage

While maintaining the Church's classical teaching about the superiority of apostolic celibacy, Opus Dei's founder did open up a new way: 'More than once I have seen the eyes of men and women light up when they heard me say that marriage is a divine path upon this earth, whereas they had thought it impossible in their case to combine the giving of oneself to God and a love which is divine, noble and pure.'

For the Christian, marriage is not simply a social institution and still less a remedy for human weakness. It is a genuine supernatural vocation, which can be sanctified in all its aspects. God has given the body the ability to share in his own creative power and has wished to use marital love to bring new beings into the world. Thus Mgr. Escrivá affirmed that sexuality 'is not something shameful; it is a divine gift whose true purpose is life, love, fertility'. With this perspective, life in the family, marital relations, the care and upbringing of children, the effort to improve the material condition of the home, relationships with other people, are just so many ordinary human situations to which Christian couples have to give a supernatural character.

Marriage and everyday life

He used to dream of 'bright and cheerful Christian homes' unaffected by the inevitable difficulties that arise, because mutual love would manage to overcome them. It is precisely when circumstances become difficult that self-giving and tenderness acquire deeper roots and really come into their own. To get across the practical implications of love between husband and wife the founder, when he received couples, would sometimes ask the husband (and similarly the wife) if he loved his spouse to the point of loving even her faults (as long as they were not offensive to God). If the reply was negative, or hesitant, he used to remark that his love was still imperfect.

Furthermore, he would tirelessly urge his listeners 'not to stem the sources of life, to have a supernatural approach, and the courage needed to bring up a large family', if God sent them one.

In his preaching Mgr. Escrivá underlined the decisive role played by parents in the education of their children, a role which they cannot hand over to others, not even to teachers, because parents educate essentially through their behaviour. He encouraged them to make sure that their children from their very earliest years could see them trying to live in accord with their faith; so that 'the child learns to have our Lord among its first affections, its basic affections; and learns to treat God as its Father and our Lady as its Mother'.

Respecting the vocation of one's children

The founder described the fourth commandment, to honour one's parents, as 'the sweetest precept of the Decalogue'.

However, a son or daughter's freedom and duties can sometimes run counter to parents' wishes. Parents should act as guides; they have a right to advise their children on their career choice, professional life, and on their choice of a state in life; but they should also respect whatever vocation God may give a child of theirs. Christians who are trying to sanctify themselves as husbands or wives and who are conscious of the greatness of their own vocation, cannot but rejoice to see their children called to live a life of apostolic celibacy.

Parents ought to fight any temptation to project their own ambitions on to their children or to impose a preconceived plan on their lives. When Catholic parents fail to understand the vocation of giving oneself to the service of God and to souls, they have, in Mgr. Escrivá's mind 'failed in their mission to form a Christian family; they are not even aware of the dignity Christianity gives to their matrimonial vocation'.

On the other hand, he was convinced that most children owe their vocation to their parents. He explained it like this: 'If you had brought them up to be like criminals, they would be in prison. You have brought them up to be children of God, and God has taken them from you. He has accepted them.'

PRIESTHOOD AND HOLINESS

Dignity of the priesthood

Throughout his life Mgr. Escrivá took an extraordinary interest in the welfare of priests, in view of their great influence for good or evil. He spared no effort in helping fellow priests, and in preparing some of his sons for the priesthood. In his lifetime he himself led over one thousand men to the priesthood.

Through the sacrament of Orders, a priest is able 'to lend our Lord his voice, his hands, his whole being', celebrating the Holy Mass *in persona Christi*, in the person of Christ, and being the direct and everyday instrument of the salvific grace won for us by Christ on the Cross. He is a special intermediary between God and man, and the means by which man is sanctified. However, he ought not to forget that he himself is also called to sanctity, just as lay people are.

Mission of the priest

Without in any way putting himself forward as an example, Mgr. Escrivá said of himself that he was a priest who spoke only of God. He felt this was the basic mission of every priest. As for members's of Opus Dei who were ordained after years of ordinary, nine to five jobs, he used to remind them that they had become priests to serve, and not to stand out or to give orders. Once they were priests they would leave their old profession behind and devote themselves entirely to their new 'professional work' to which 'they will dedicate every hour of the day, and still be short of time'.

While making clear that he did not know any bad priests (at most there were some who were a little 'unwell'), the founder did say how he regretted that there were 'some priests who instead of speaking about God, (which is all they ought to be talking about) speak about politics, sociology and anthropology. Since they know nothing about these things they get it wrong, and moreover, our Lord is not happy with this. A priest's ministry consists, instead, in preaching the teaching of Jesus Christ and administering the sacraments, helping people to see Christ, to love Christ, to follow Christ. Anything else is outside their province.' This is the only way for the priest to steer clear of rival factions; to act otherwise would be to betray Christ, and to build a 'new' Church, substituting temporal goals for supernatural goals, thus losing the respect and obedience of the people and destroying the Church from the inside.

Conclusion

I hope that this short survey of Opus Dei makes it easier to understand both its doctrine and the lifestyle of its members.

Opus Dei would never have become a spiritual catalyst in the modern world were it not for the extraordinary personality God gave Mgr. Escrivá who, faithful to divine inspiration, 'sculptured' its spirit right down to the last detail.

For Cardinal Koenig of Vienna 'Mgr. Escrivá de Balaguer belongs to that select number of apostles, prophets, evangelists, pastors, teachers ...' (cf. Eph 4:11) who have contributed in a remarkable way to the building up of the Body of Christ. The profound humanity of the founder of Opus Dei reflects the character and concerns of our time.

But his charisma – that of someone set apart to carry out a special 'work of God' – raised him to a higher plane; it projected him into the future. That is why he anticipated what were to be the great pastoral themes of the Church on the eve of the third millennium of its history.

Furthermore, if in this changing world, Opus Dei remains exactly as the Founder saw it on 2 October 1928, it is because its members, all with the same vocation to holiness and apostolate in the middle of the world, strive to maintain a unity of spirit, to be one with their Prelate, and to make their own the on-going spiritual training which is part of their commitment.

Rather than by reading the works listed in the bibliography, it is through direct contact with the founder and members of Opus Dei that one can appreciate this solidarity.

It would not perhaps be too presumptuous to suggest that we are witnessing one of those silent revolutions of which the Holy Spirit holds the secret. The ecclesial importance and social implications of Opus Dei are just beginning to emerge. Only time will show its full significance, especially since, as Mgr. Escrivá said:

'Opus Dei will never have any problems of adapting to the world because its members are in the world; it will never have to catch up with human progress precisely because it is these very members, side by side with other men and women living in the world, who bring about this progress by their *everyday work.*'

Short Bibliography on Opus Dei

BOOKS

P. Bristow, *Opus Dei* (Catholic Truth Society, London 2001)

H. Scott & E. Tolanski, *Josemaría Escrivá* (Catholic Truth Society, London 2001)

A. Vazquez de Prada, *The Founder of Opus Dei, Volume I: The Early Years* (Scepter, Princeton 2001)

V. Messori, *Opus Dei: Leadership and Vision in Today's Catholic Church* (Regnery, Washington DC 1997)

A. del Portillo, *Immersed in God* (Scepter, Princeton 1996)

G. Romano, *Opus Dei: Who, How, Why* (Alba House, New York 1995)

P. Rodriguez, F. Ocariz, J. L. Illanes, *Opus Dei in the Church* (Four Courts, Dublin 1994)

A. de Fuenmayor, V. Gomez-Iglesias, J. L. Illanes, *The Canonical Path of Opus Dei: The History and Defence of a Charism* (Scepter-MTF, Chicago 1994)

P. Berglar, *Opus Dei: Life and Work of Its Founder* (Scepter, Princeton 1993)

F. Gondrand, *At God's Pace* (Scepter, New York 1989)

D. Helming, *Footprints in the Snow* (Scepter, New York 1986)

S. Bernal, *Mgr. J. Escrivá: A Profile of the Founder of Opus Dei* (Scepter, London 1977)

ARTICLES AND BOOKLETS

General

Opus Dei – a Personal Prelature (Sinag Tala, Manila 1983)

R. Farrell, 'Opus Dei: Separating the facts from the fiction', *Flourish*, Glasgow, May 1985

J. Flader, 'Personal Prelatures of Opus Dei', *Australasian Catholic Record*, Vol. LX, no. 4, 1983

A. de Fuenmayor, 'La Ereccion del Opus Dei en Prelatura Personal', *Ius Canonicum*, XXIII, 1983

G. Haddock, 'Work sanctifies human environment', *Catholic Register*, Toronto 1984

P. Harman, 'Opus Dei's Ideal: A Saint in the world', *Irish Catholic*, Dublin 1984

D. M. Helming, *Christianity for everyman* (Scepter, Chicago 1972)

J. Horrigan, 'Opus Dei: Its ideals and the unseen influence', *The Times*, London, 23 January 1981

W. Keenan, 'What is the truth of Opus Dei?', *Universe*, London, 30 January 1981

J. R. Madurga, 'The Laity in the Opus Dei Prelature', *Catholic Position Papers*, Ashiya 1984

M. Polak, 'Serving the Church in the midst of the world', *The Advocate*, Melbourne 1984

U. Poletti, 'Decree for the Introduction of the Cause of Beatification and Canonization of the Servant of God, Mgr. Josemaría Escrivá de Balaguer', *Newsletter* No. 4, 1982

P. Rodriguez, *The Way: A spirituality of Christian Life* (Scepter, New York 1974)

G. W. Rutler, 'The Rise of Opus Dei', *Position Papers*, Dublin, November 1983

M. and T. Shannon, *Christianity in everyday life* (Catholic Truth Society, Australia 1979)

R. Shaw, 'The Secret of Opus Dei, *Columbia* (New Haven, 1982)

W. H. Stetson, 'Opus Dei: the first personal Prelature', *Homiletic and Pastoral Review* (New York, July 1983)

G. Thibon, 'La sainteté du quotidien', *Le Figaro* (Paris 1976)

G. Wheeler, 'Christianising the civilisation of our times', *Scottish Catholic Observer*, Glasgow, 23 April 1982

By Cardinals

L. Aponte, *El Visitante de Puerto Rico*, 11 February 1979; S. Baggio, *The Priest*, Indiana, March 1976; S. Baggio, *L'Osservatore Romano*, Vatican City, 17 January 1983; J. J. Carberry, *The Priest*, Indiana, June 1979; M. Casariego, *L'Osservatore Romano*, 14 July 1979; T. Cooke, *The Catholic News*, New York, 28 September 1978; D. I. Ekandem, *Independent*, Ibadan, 25 March 1978; R. Etchegaray, *Le Figaro*, Paris, 31 August 1981; J. Hoeffner, *Palabra*, Madrid, October 1979; F. Koenig, *Catholic Weekly*, 20 June 1984; F. Koenig, *L'Osservatore Romano*, 23 June 1985; G. Lecaro, *Corriere della Sera*, Milan, 25 June 1976; A. Luciani, *Il Gazzettino*, Venice, 25 July 1978; H. Medieros, *National Catholic Register*, Los Angeles, 2 July 1978; M. Otunga, *Sunday Nation*, Nairobi, 3 February 1980; V. Parente, *L'Osservatore Romano*, Vatican City, 24 June 1979; U. Poletti, *Rivista diocesana di Roma*, July/August 1977; A. Rossi, *O Estado de Sao Paolo*, 27 June 1976; J. Sin, *Bulletin Today*, Manila, 29 June 1976; C. Urio, *Il Mattino*, Naples, 26 June 1979.

Encyclopaedias

'Opus Dei' in *Gran Enciclopedia Rialp* (Madrid); *The Europa Year Book* (London); *Guida Monaci* (Rome); *Verbo Enciclopeia Luso-Brasileira de Cultura* (Lisbon); 'Mgr. Escrivá' in *Gran Enciclopedia Rialp* (Madrid); *International Who's Who* (London); Dictionary of International Biography (Cambridge); *Who's Who in the World* (Chicago); 'Mgr. A. del Portillo' in *Gran Enciclopedia Rialp* (Madrid); *International Who's Who* (London); *Men of Achievement* (Cambridge); *Dictionary of International Biography* (Cambridge); *Who's Who in the World* (Chicago).

WRITINGS OF THE FOUNDER OF OPUS DEI

Consideraciones espirituales (1934)

Holy Rosary (1934): now published in 23 languages, with a total of 700,000 copies printed.

The Way (1939): 42 languages; four million copies.

La Abadesa de las Huelgas (1944)

Conversations with Mgr. Escrivá (1968): 9 languages; 350,000 copies.

Christ is Passing By (1973): 13 languages; 450,000 copies.

Friends of God (1977): 13 languages; 400,000 copies.

The Way of the Cross (1981): 18 languages; 400,000 copies.

In Love with the Church (1986): 8 languages; 40,000 copies.

Furrow (1986): 18 languages; 450,000 copies.

The Forge (1987): 12 languages; 400,000 copies.